Winner's Guide to
SEGA® GENESIS®

Kate Barnes

HAYDEN BOOKS
A Division of Howard W. Sams & Company
11711 North College, Suite 141, Carmel, IN 46032 USA

@1990 by Kate Barnes

FIRST EDITION
FIRST PRINTING—1990

All rights reserved. No part of this book shall be reproduced, stored in a retrieval system, or transmitted by any means, electronic, mechanical, photocopying, recording, or otherwise, without written permission from the publisher. No patent liability is assumed with respect to the use of the information contained herein. While every precaution has been taken in the preparation of this book, the publisher and author assume no responsibility for errors or omissions. Neither is any liability assumed for damages resulting from the use of the information contained herein.

International Standard Book Number: 0-672-48489-7
Library of Congress Catalog Card Number: 90-61219

Acquisitions Editor: *Marie Butler-Knight*
Manuscript Editor: *Sara Black*
Production Coordinator: *Becky Imel*
Designer: *Glenn Santner*
Illustrator: *Tami Hughes*
Cover Artist: *Keith J. Hampton*
Production Assistance: *Claudia Bell, Sally Copenhaver, Denny Hager, Sharon Hilgenberg, Charles Hutchinson, Lori Lyons, Jennifer Matthews, Dennis Sheehan, Mary Beth Wakefield*

Printed in the United States of America

Contents

Introduction, v

Part

one

Genesis Games

Alex Kidd in the Enchanted Castle, 3
Altered Beasts, 13
Arnold Palmer Tournament Golf, 19
Ghouls'n Ghosts, 27
Golden Axe, 35
Last Battle, 43
Rambo III, 49
Super Hang-On, 57
The Revenge of Shinobi, 65
Thunder Force II, 73
Tommy Lasorda Baseball, 83
World Championship Soccer, 91
Zoom!, 97

Part two

Master System Games

Alex Kidd in Miracle World, 107
Phantasy Star, 115
R-Type, 123
Reggie Jackson Baseball, 131
Shinobi, 137
Wonder Boy in Monster Land, 143

Introduction

Hot. That's the word for Sega Genesis games. The Genesis system has fearsome beasts, fast bikes, and free-for-all battles. You can pick up most games and have some success immediately. Few can be completely mastered quickly. Tricky maneuvers and hidden remedies abound. The challenge of Sega games means you'll have plenty of hours of play with any single game. And, with *Winner's Guide to Sega Genesis* you'll be able to play better, faster. Overall strategies and specific tips help you get the most out of your game time.

You can play Sega Master System games on your Genesis equipment. (I've covered the best and most popular in this book.) However, for the real sound, graphic, speed, thrill bonanza, go for the games made just for Genesis.

This book contains descriptions of popular Genesis games and top-selling Master System games. The Master System was Sega's earlier, 8-bit system while Genesis is Sega's super-duper 16-bit system. You'll see the Genesis difference in the graphics and sophistication of play. Don't throw away your Master System games, however. By purchasing a Power Base Converter at around $30.00, you can play Master System games on your Genesis unit. (Unfortunately, there is no way to play Genesis games on a Master System. The power just isn't there.) Many of the Master System games are plenty of fun and the Power Base Converter works fine.

If you've played Sega games (in an arcade or on a home system), you'll know they're not simple. Some of the strategies can be studied for hours that turn into months if not years. This book can't cover all the tips in all situations, so I went for capturing the *best* strategies and *most useful* tips.

Since there's more than one way to skin a game, two imaginary game characters talk about their approaches. Throughout the book, you'll see the strategies of Hi and Tec, a dynamic duo who don't always agree. You'll see that Hi and Tec tend to focus on different aspects of the games.

For those of you who rent or borrow (versus buy) games, you may not get the helpful manual Sega packs with each game. Just for you, the basic mechanics of each game and use of the controller are summarized. Remember that you must have the machine off each time you swap cartridges (or you'll be flirting with wearing out a cartridge).

I hope the approaches of Hi and Tec help improve your play. If you discover strategies or tips of your own, send them to me in care of the publisher. Your name will be mentioned in the next edition if your pointers are used.

Acknowledgments

Thanks to Jeffery Cochran and Jonathan Olawski for tips and tolerence of general life disruption. Bless Squidley for waiting for dinner.

Trademark Acknowledgments

All terms mentioned in this book that are known to be trademarks or service marks are listed below. In addition, terms suspected of being trademarks or service marks have been appropriately capitalized.

Introduction

Howard W. Sams & Company cannot attest to the accuracy of this information. Use of a term in this book should not be regarded as affecting the validity of any trademark or service mark.

Alex Kidd in Miracle World is a trademark of Sega.

Alex Kidd in the Enchanted Castle is a trademark of Sega.

Altered Beasts is a trademark of Sega.

Arnold Palmer Tournament Golf is a trademark of Sega.

Ghouls'n Ghosts is a trademark of Capcom and was reprogrammed by Sega.

Golden Axe is a trademark of Sega.

Last Battle is a trademark of Sega.

Phantasy Star is a trademark of Sega.

R-Type is a trademark of IREM Corp and was reprogrammed by Sega.

Reggie Jackson Baseball is a trademark of Sega.

Shinobi is a trademark of Sega.

Super Hang On is a trademark of CarolCo Pictures, Inc. and Sega.

The Revenge of Shinobi is a trademark of Sega.

Thunder Force II is a trademark of Techno Soft.

Tommy Lasorda Baseball is a trademark of Sega.

Wonder Boy in Monster Land is a trademark of Sega and Sega/Westone.

World Championship Soccer is a trademark of Sega.

Zoom! is a trademark of Discovery Software and Sega.

Part

one

Genesis Games

Alex Kidd in the Enchanted Castle

Description

If you've played other Sega Alex Kidd games, you'll be immediately familiar with this one. Alex's father, King Thor, is AWOL. Alex leaves Aries and goes to Paperock to find his father. He punches, jumps, and kicks his way through his quest and plays the game of paper-rock-scissors. Alex needs your help because the path is peppered with jokers and misbehaving misfits.

Let's Play

The following buttons give you overall control of the game. Use them to control Alex as he wanders and plunders.

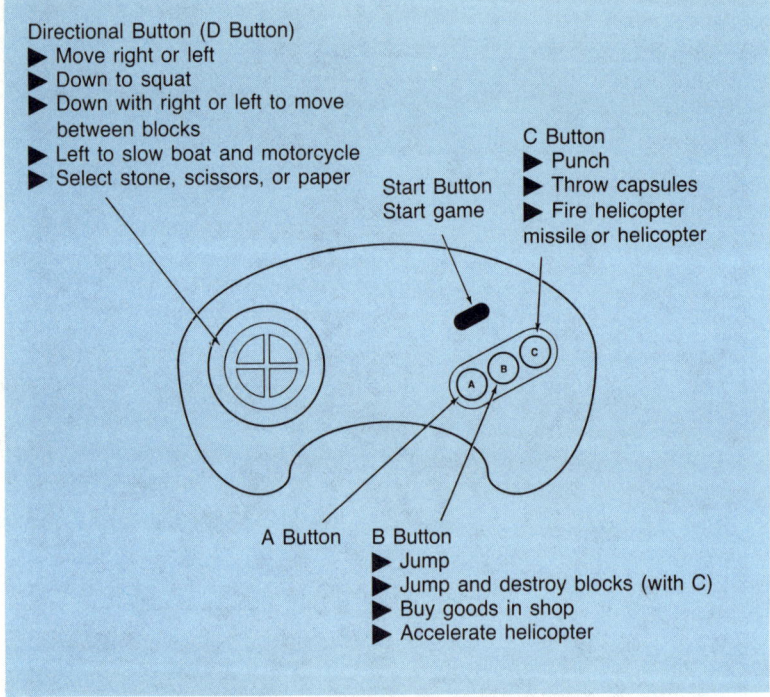

Directional Button (D Button)
- Move right or left
- Down to squat
- Down with right or left to move between blocks
- Left to slow boat and motorcycle
- Select stone, scissors, or paper

Start Button
Start game

C Button
- Punch
- Throw capsules
- Fire helicopter missile or helicopter

A Button

B Button
- Jump
- Jump and destroy blocks (with C)
- Buy goods in shop
- Accelerate helicopter

Through the Options screen, you can control the following game characteristics:

- *Continue* begins a new game in the round where you last stopped (assuming you have 1,000 Baums of gold).

- *Difficulty* sets the number of lives and determines how sordid the villains are. Easy gives you five lives, Normal allows three lives, and Hard permits only one.

- *Control* allows you to change the A, B, and C Buttons like this:

Setting	A & C Buttons	B Button
Normal	Jump	Punch
Reverse	Punch	Jump

- *Sound Test* previews a sound (use the A or C Button) and choose a new sound.

- *Janken* lets you practice the paper-rock-scissors game against the opponent of your choice. Paper wraps rock; rocks break scissors; scissors cut paper.

This game has eleven rounds. You must grab a triangular rice cake when you finish each round. The rounds are:

- *Round 1:* Rookietown (your town) where you go for the gold

- *Round 2:* Prairie where you can forget about the curled-up hedge hogs

- *Round 3:* Splashy Sea where you can kill the octopus tentacle by tentacle

- *Round 4:* Scorpion Desert where there is all kind of trouble

- *Round 5:* Pyramid where there are mummies and scorpions

- *Round 6:* Hiho Forest where you can say hello to manic monkeys and other crazy creatures

- *Round 7:* Tropics Town where you travel under palm trees—but this is no South Sea vacation

- *Round 8:* Rocky Mountain #1 where you maneuver across a tension bridge

- *Round 9:* Rocky Mountain #2 where you climb and avoid stones sent your way by the Old Wizard

- *Round 10:* The Sky where you'll certainly want your Pedicopter
- *Round 11:* Sky Castle where you control suspended ceilings and battle other villains to find your father

Check out the chests for treasures and a few ringers. The treasures include gold coins worth 10 Baums each, bags of gold worth 100 Baums each, tokens that allow you to read the minds of those with whom you play Janken, and extra lives. Watch out! Some chests include bombs.

Push the Start Button to go to the Item Selection screen. From it, pick items to assist you on your journey. These articles include:

- *Power Bracelet* — use as a weapon when walking without the Wizard's Cane.
- *Motorcycle* — use to kill you enemies. (Avoid rocks that don't break, or they'll break you.)
- *Pedicopter* — use to flit in the heavens and to fire bullets.
- *Pogo Stick* — use to bounce high.
- *Wizard's Cane* — use to temporarily move through the air.
- *Cape* — use once to be indestructible. (It does not work on lava lakes and suspended ceilings.)
- *Tokens* — use to read minds during Janken play.
- *Lives* — use to identify how many you have left.

Strategies

 **Hi's Hints**

Be careful and move slowly. If you take off bounding across the screen, you'll be in trouble.

Also be careful how you punch and kick. To jump and kick at the same time, let go of the button to get the kick. If you don't land on your foot, you will probably die and watch your ghost float off the screen.

Unlike many games, there's no time pressure. No clock is ticking. So approach the game in a slow and easy manner.

Stay high on the screen since more danger lies on the bottom of the screen. This is not true when an eagle is overhead, so stay away from the eagles.

Another effective strategy is to jump over the bad guys. Some things aren't worth trying to kill. However, jumping over bad guys doesn't work when they follow you.

For beginners, the easiest way to kill without being killed is to stand in front of the object, jump straight up in the air, and hit the directional control slightly so you land on top of the object. When you jump up, make sure that you do not bounce into something overhead that would cause you to get killed. To jump higher, use a running start.

You should develop your punching skill. A general rule is: Don't jump when a punch will do. When you jump, you don't know where you're going to land. When you throw a punch, you can always jump if the punch doesn't work.

If you need to get money, play paper-rock-scissors. Scissors works out pretty well, especially if you use it repeatedly. The game seems to think that you'll change your response. Not changing your response can give you above average returns.

Another effective strategy to use when learning the game is to play paper-rock-scissors no matter what other alternatives you might have. If you're lucky, you'll have the advantage so that you can play the game a third time (if you don't think you'll have the necessary 1,000 points to get out of the round). If you think you'll have your 1,000 points, then decline the offer so you don't lose any money.

Getting the chests is financially rewarding. They are loaded with money and powers. The bags are better than the coins since the bags are worth more. The coins are hard to handle. They run on the ground, and you can't pick them up when they're flat. Try for the golden chests rather than the red ones. The golden chests usually have extra powers, although they sometimes contain bombs.

Whenever you punch or kick a treasure chest, stay there for a moment. The money will materialize quickly. If you see or even suspect a bomb, move away as fast as possible to save your life. If you fall off a chest, you won't be able to get back in time to get your reward.

The special chest frequently appears to be locked in solid rock. Usually, you will have to jump or punch the rock to get the chest.

Tec's Tips

To get started, let's take a look at the typical types of action you see in some of the rounds.

In the first two rounds, there's a hidden underground cavern. It is under the palm tree in Round 1 and under the pile of blue marbles topped by a gold chest in Round 2. When you jump and take a divot out of the ground, jump again on that spot and the nearby area to go down into the cavern. Here you'll find treasures, including money. But danger lurks. You may have to give up a life, but it can be worth the risk to get the money.

Press the D Button up in Round 3 to jump back to the world above the water. Be sure to find out what's going on above the water before you jump. Staying up isn't easy, but remember that you can land on something undesirable if you go back under the water. The octopus in this round is too tough to mess with since you have to kill all its tentacles. I swim around it. At the end of Round 3, you need 1,000 Baums of gold to get out. Try to get them early so you can concentrate on finishing the round.

Round 4 features several different kinds of rocks. You can punch, move, and build things out of brown rocks. The gray-looking ones are lumps; you can't do anything with them. Use the black rocks to help you bounce higher. You don't have to jump. Just center yourself over one, and it will do all the bouncing for you.

The crazy condors first appear in Round 2 and then again in Round 4. They are bothersome. You just have to wait until they fly away before you can do anything. The condors protect a land of treasures that hovers high above the desert.

When you get to the levels with the balls, you can punch the balls to take out some barriers. When you're around the bouncy rocks, spring off them to get somewhere you otherwise couldn't go.

In Round 5, you can't avoid some of the villains (such as mummies and scorpions) that you could duck in previous rounds. You have to kill them. At the beginning of this round, go through the lower level of the pyramid and kill the first mummy that you see. Then you can go the back way to see what's in the treasure chest.

The Queen of the Oasis at the end of Round 5 challenges you with rock-paper-scissors. I use three scissors in a row to get her to say, "I can't believe it!" You'll get your own strategy for dealing with her and the other bosses that appear at the end of each round.

Since you have to get a running start to jump long distances, knock a few blocks out of the way to make a longer running path. This is especially useful to get past the double scorpions at the end of some levels.

More Power Pointers

- When you lose a life, you give up the treasure you were using.
- You rarely die from falling.
- Coins in high treasure chests will bounce higher than coins in lower chests. Bags of money never bounce. They stay right where they are.
- Watch out for villains that hang out under overhead areas. They want you to jump and hit them.
- Be alert to villains that travel in pairs. If you kill one of them and then go for the coin, the odds are that the other one will kill you.

Manufacturer Information

Company: Sega of America, Inc.

Address: P.O. Box 2167
South San Francisco, CA
94080

Game Counselor Hot Line: 415-871-GAME
(Please remember this is a regular toll charge telephone call.) 6 a.m. to 8:45 p.m. Pacific Time Monday through Friday and 8 a.m. to 5:45 p.m. Pacific Time Saturday and Sunday

Typical Price: $39.99

Altered Beast

Description

You are a dead Roman Centurion. You have been summoned from the dead to become the Altered Beast—a man with many personalities. You'll need each one of them. In these trying times, enemies of all sorts are likely to surprise you.

Here's the main plot. After you are once again filled with life, you're determined to find and fight Neff (the god of the Underworld). Chivalry is at the root of your search. Athena, the daughter of Zeus, must be freed so that she can take her place among the gods.

Let's Play

The following buttons give you overall control of the game. Use them to control the Roman Centurion, which is your form at the beginning of each round. Once you evolve into a beast, you will use the A, B, and C Buttons differently as described later.

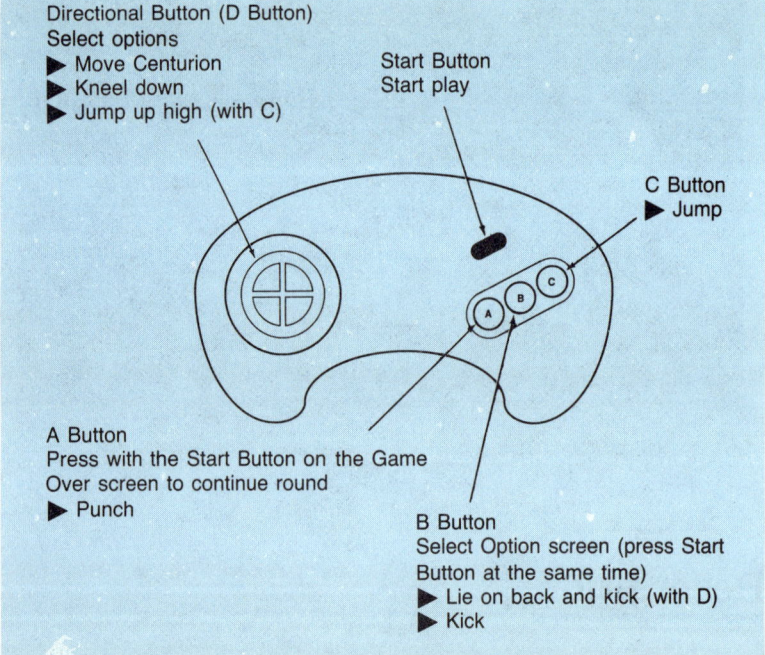

Once you become the Altered Beast in each of five rounds, these are your forms and powers:

- *Round 1—Werewolf:* The A Button allows you to shoot fireballs from your arm, while the B Button moves you forward like a streak of flame.

- *Round 2—Weredragon:* The A Button shoots lightening from your arm, and the B Button shields you in a protective laser barrier.

- *Round 3—Werebear:* The A Button gives you bad bear breath that turns enemies to stone, while the B Button makes you spin and blow like a madman.

- Round 4—Weretiger: The A Button flings balls of flame from your fingers, and the B Button allows you to send masses of fire up and down.

- Round 5—Gold Werewolf: The A Button allows you to throw golden fire, and the B Button allows you to send surges of golden fire.

Your life gauge (at the top of the screen) identifies the number of lives left. The power gauge (at the bottom of the screen) shows your energy level. When you lose your power gauge, a life goes away. You cannot liberate Athena without lives.

For a better fighting chance, use the Option screen to set the level of difficulty, increase your power gauge and the number of lives you have, or change the round of the game.

The key to this game is capturing the spirit balls that come when you destroy a three-headed wolf. If you touch the spirit ball, you'll receive its alchemic power. At the beginning, before you become the Altered Beast, you get progressively bigger.

Occasionally, Neff himself appears as a draped man to fight you. You can get bonus points if you beat him, but he's a tough competitor and should be avoided.

Strategies

 ### Hi's Hints

I view Altered Beast as a distance game. I've experimented with the distance between me and each of my combatants. For example, the Slow Feet enemies (the ones you meet first) are very easy to defeat. You can get close to them and punch them; they aren't particularly dangerous. As you move on, however, you meet creatures with longer arms, creatures that punch back, and those with powerful punches. Then it becomes critical to know the distance that is both safe and effective.

In addition to distance, you must identify the proper strategy to use. You can punch, and you can kick. You can also jump and punch, jump and kick, or lie on your back and kick (press the D Button). Don't underestimate the usefulness of jumping or ducking while striking. Jumping also gives you a new angle of attack.

For instance, you want to contact the spirit balls that come from the blue (not brown) three-headed wolves. The best way to kill a blue three-headed wolf is to kick it. If a blue three-headed wolf is above you, I've found that I can lie on my back and kick it.

The spirit ball will usually come to you. Occasionally, it will begin to float upward. When it does, don't forget that you can jump to capture it.

It's also important to determine which creatures are best to avoid and which are best to attack. With a few exceptions, all creatures are good for attacking. The round leaches in Round 2 are dangerous; however, they're worth a lot of points. You should also avoid the rock turtles, which move slowly in Round 3. When you approach a creature, weigh the points you get against the danger each represents to determine who to attack first. Also, if you know the typical behavior of an enemy, you can better anticipate what the enemy will do.

Play the game in the easier, practice level first. This way you can explore the strategies and get to know the different types of enemies without having to deal with too many of them. Don't be too hasty to jump to the last round. The enemies in this game are cumulative. You meet all of them in the last level, and you won't survive long unless you have some experience.

When you have mastered the basics, try playing with a partner. When you play together on the professional level, you'll have twice the killing power.

Altered Beasts

Tec's Tips

As I play, I keep track of the amount of energy I have. Each time I'm hit, I lose energy. The amount of energy you lose depends on the type of enemy. The amount of energy you have can be controlled on the Option screen.

When you become any "werebeast," you get special powers. For example, in Round 2 you can become the weredragon and can move up and down and hang in the air.

With different fighting powers, you have different strength. So you may have to punch more than once. You may want to reserve some of the special fighting power for a particularly deadly enemy.

At the end of each level, you get a bonus. But, you have to return all your energy and start working at the beginning of the level to become the next werebeast. With time, you'll get increasingly better as the rounds get tougher.

More Power Pointers

- When you first encounter a new, evil creature, try using the B Button. It usually has a more powerful striking ability than the A Button.

- Become a werebeast in each round before you attempt to defeat the boss at the end of the round. You need the "were" power, a knowledge of weak points, a strategy to move, and a store of energy when you meet the boss.

Manufacturer Information

Company: Sega of America, Inc.

Address: P.O. Box 2167
South San Francisco, CA
94080

Game Counselor Hot Line: 415-871-GAME
(Please remember this is a regular toll charge telephone call.) 6 a.m. to 8:45 p.m. Pacific Time Monday through Friday and 8 a.m. to 5:45 p.m. Pacific Time Saturday and Sunday

Typical Price: Free with Genesis system

Arnold Palmer Tournament Golf

Description

It's tee time, and this is not your local par three for beginners. Welcome to three 18-hole courses. Play alone, with a companion, in a tourney, in match play, or just for practice.

The object is to sink the ball in the hole with as few shots as possible. It sounds easy, but you must choose your clubs, control your swing, improve your skill, listen to your caddy, watch the wind, and avoid the traps. All the factors that make golf exciting come into play in Arnold Palmer Tournament Golf. You have only 100 shots on a course. There is no such thing as a tie. Sudden death takes care of that. And if you win, Arnie will be proud.

Let's Play

The following buttons give you overall control of the game. Use them to control your golf game.

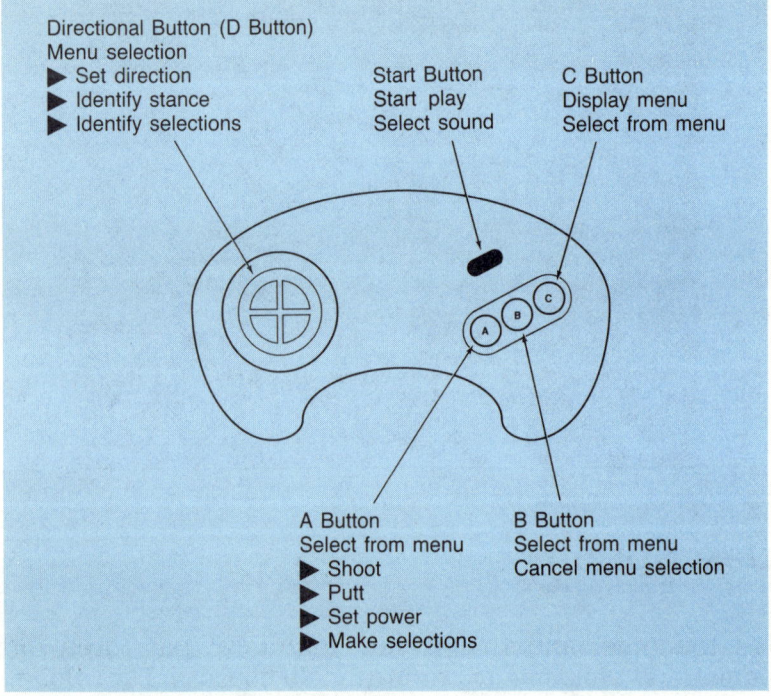

This game has many options when you get started. At the title screen, press the Start Button to see the Game Select screen. You'll see: Tournament and Practice. After you select you options, pick End and press the Start Button for the next screen.

In Tournament play, it's you and 15 other players in 12 rounds of golf. Rounds 7 and 11 are match rather than stroke play. In the Tournament game, you must get in the top eight to up your distance in the shot, improve your shots, and get better caddy counsel. Select New Game to start. You may then enter your name, read about tournament play, change the clubs Sega selects for you, and see winners and their earnings.

Tournament play also has a Password option. You'll see a password at the end of each round. If you want to break for a commercial, remember the password, quit, then use the Password option to resume play. Press the Start Button to skip any introductory screens and, finally, to tee off. When you enter the password, identify each letter with the D Button, press the A, B, or C Button to select a letter, then identify End and press the A, B, or C Button followed by the Start Button to go again.

Under the Practice heading on the Game Select screen, you may play a stroke game for one or two players. Enter your name, select club materials and clubs, the level (difficulty, power, skill, and caddy counsel), and the course.

Another Practice option is Match Play. This is a hole-for-hole game. If you win the most holes, you win the match. Enter your name and then pick your clubs and materials, the level, and the course.

The Practice/Practice option is for the beginning or noncompetitive player. There are no winners or losers. Enter your name and select clubs and materials. Then, set up the course your way including the holes, course, wind velocity and direction, and expertise required. You can make the course as hard or easy as you like.

Before you swing, press the A Button repeatedly to see the weather, the position of the ball on the green, your choice of club (press the D Button then the A Button to change clubs), and your stance (press the D Button to change it).

During play, a Command menu appears. You may see your caddy's advice, the green, or the score. To swing, press the A Button three times. The first press activates the power gauge, the second press freezes the strength of the swing, and the third press identifies the height of the swing and completes the swing. On a putt, press only the A Button since there is no need to determine height.

Strategies

 ### Hi's Hints

Don't be discouraged when the rest of the field takes off ahead of you. This game is harder than the scoreboard makes it appear. With practice, you too can get birdies.

Putting is my strength. You should putt around a while to get used to the speed of the ball and the touch of the clubs. Otherwise, it'll will be frustrating and you'll play too many holes before you acquire a successful touch.

I just tap the controller on short putts. To go a couple yards, I may tap it a few times. Don't be too aggressive on the green. You'll find that the putter hits the ball very far.

I try to stay out of trouble on the fairway because the game is very generous with pitches around the green. If you have your pitching wedge set up and you're in the rough just around the green, you can press the controller several times and get a reasonably good shot.

When you're in the rough around the green, you can putt, but you must look at your lie. If the ball is lying down in the grass, the game will not be nice to you. If, on the other hand, the ball is sitting high and you're in the first cut of rough around the green, you can putt. It's also easy to chip in using your pitching wedge from the first cut of rough.

Arnold Palmer Tournament Golf

Tec's Tips

Watch the wind! If there's a wind, it will always influence your shot.

To land in the fairway consistently, look ahead to see the flag. Line up on the edge of the sand bunkers. Stay just a little out of the edge and don't forget to take the wind into account.

After the wind, watch the water. On most early rounds, the water loves to take the shot (especially off the tee). If you do get into a water hazard, take the drop over the replay because the distance will work for you.

As you plan the shot, don't be afraid to aim way out to the right or way out to the left even though it's off the screen. If you move the arrow far enough, it will let you look at a different part of the hole. On several holes it's a good idea not to aim anywhere in the picture that appears when you first come up to the hole.

Turn your feet to the right and your ball will curve left. Turn your feet to the left and your ball will curve right. Don't develop this as a bad habit or your shot will always look like a banana. Just use the technique when you're behind an obstacle or when there is a strong wind blowing left or right so you can cut the ball into the wind.

I find that most of the strokes are lost around the green or in the hazards. You need to play smart. For example, when you are in the bushes and the game suggests you have an unplayable lie, believe it. If you try to hit the ball, the game will never give it to you. The smart thing to do is go to the advice option and take your unplayable lie.

To get maximum power, set the power gauge all the way to the top. If you are late and the gauge tops out, you get no shot. It's as if it was a practice swing. Learn how to wait until the power on the gauge gets to the end. This way, you'll get maximum power.

Practice with the gauge. For example, the pitching wedge will go 100 yards. Therefore, if you divide the scale into 100 yards (and if there's no wind) you can get very accurate in terms of hitting it 50 or 60 or 70 yards.

A relatively good strategy on the really long holes, which you can never get to in two strokes, is to choose a club so that you're about 100 yards away on your approach shot. That's a full pitching wedge, and the game is very generous about putting you near the hole.

This game is fun when you have an afternoon. You can come back and play it several times during the day and work your way through the courses in the tournament. If you can finish even par or under par in any of the tournaments, you should be proud of yourself and you'll make some money. It is also a real kick to get the blue jacket, listen to that Scottish tune, and watch them clean up the clubhouse after your big win.

More Power Pointers

- Believe it or not, you can hit the driver off the fairway. Hit two drivers back to back on those long par fours.

- It's not unusual to use an iron off the tee and then the driver off the fairway.

- Any time that you want to speed the game up (when it's giving you a review of the results or when it's giving the coffee break after nine holes), just press the A Button one or two times so you can get on with golf.

Manufacturer Information

Company: Sega of America, Inc.

Address: P.O. Box 2167
South San Francisco, CA
94080

Game Counselor Hot Line: 415-871-GAME
(Please remember this is a regular toll charge telephone call.) 6 a.m. to 8:45 p.m. Pacific Time Monday through Friday and 8 a.m. to 5:45 p.m. Pacific Time Saturday and Sunday

Typical Price: $54.99

Ghouls'n Ghosts

Description

Journey into the land of yore where knights are noble and princesses and hamlets need to be rescued. Go forth, Sir Arthur, and free the princess and avenge the borough. Thy courage in the line of duty will be tested en route with foes both natural and unnatural. Be hearty and the king's speed be with thee.

Let's Play

The following buttons give you overall control of the game. Use them to control Sir Arthur's movement and weapon firing.

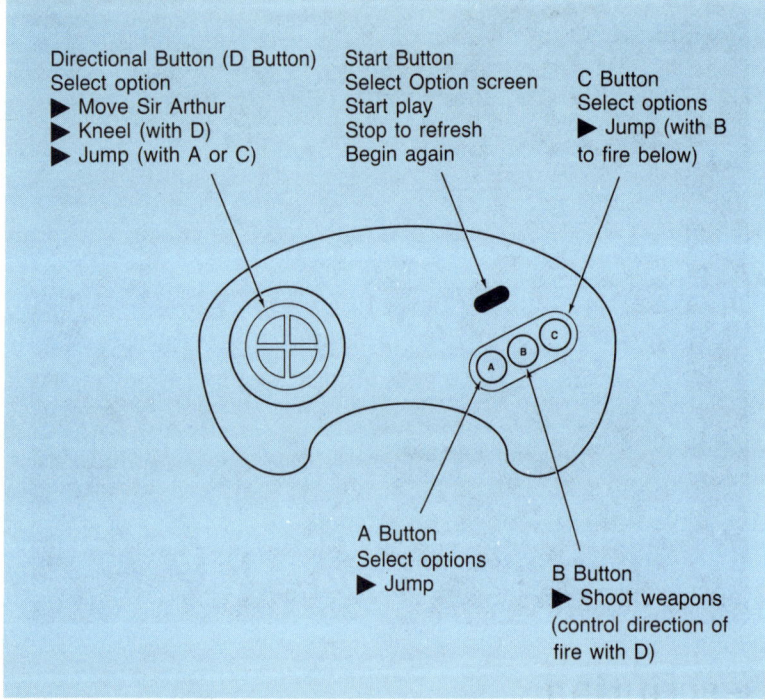

Directional Button (D Button)
Select option
▶ Move Sir Arthur
▶ Kneel (with D)
▶ Jump (with A or C)

Start Button
Select Option screen
Start play
Stop to refresh
Begin again

C Button
Select options
▶ Jump (with B to fire below)

A Button
Select options
▶ Jump

B Button
▶ Shoot weapons (control direction of fire with D)

In the menu, you may select one of 26 tunes, the level of difficulty (either Practice or Professional), the Joy Stick option (whether to go diagonally with the D Button as in an arcade), player control (1 or 2 players), sound (1 to listen in and 2 for no sound), and pad control (1 or 2 players).

The gist of your joust is this: Sir Arthur has three lives shielded by a coat of armor. When he is hit, his armor falls off. With the next affliction, he becomes a skeleton and loses a life. He will also lose a life if he does not pass quickly enough through the end gateway of a level (2:30 minutes in the first-stage levels and 3 minutes in the other levels). Save time to fight the nasty boss protecting the gate. Lives are gained with points.

Ghouls'n Ghosts has five stages of play with these levels:

- *Stage 1/Level 1:* As Sir Arthur, you embark on the journey from the deep and dark Execution Place. Avoid death and vultures.

- *Stage 1/Level 2:* You must battle wind and rain to cross the lake.

- *Stage 2/Level 1:* At the Village of Decay, pass the windmill. If you fall in the gorge, you may not return.

- *Stage 2/Level 2:* Thunder and lightning is nothing compared to the Town of Fire.

- *Stage 3/Level 1:* Is the princess in Baron Rankel's Tower? No, but watch out for what is there.

- *Stage 3/Level 2:* The Horrible Faced Mountain awaits you. Crossing the tongue of the mountain is the way to the princess.

- *Stage 4/Level 1:* The Crystal Forest leads to the Demon's Castle. It's beautiful, but don't touch it.

- *Stage 5:* Rescue the princess and rescue yourself.

The top of the screen indicates your score, the top score, and the time. The current weapon appears in a moving box under Sir Arthur. The number of lives available is in the lower right corner. The lower left corner displays the number of magic powers (if Sir Arthur has been heroic enough to acquire them).

Weapons and speed are the means to survival. Touch a weapon and it's yours. When the magic gauge turns silver, touch the magic suit of armor for magical powers. There are the six weapons:

Sword: You must toss it straight. (Magic: Throws torpedoes up, left, or right.)

Big Axe: Because it is large, it is difficult to throw, especially low, but it can hack through objects. (Magic: Explodes near objects.)

Super Sword: You can't toss it, but it is very sturdy and sharp. (Magic: Summons the Thunder Dragon to demolish all in the sky.)

Fire Water: It fans blue flames, although you must shoot it early. Unfortunately, it is bulky and doesn't go far. (Magic: Protected by fireballs.)

Discus: It brushes the ground (even over hills). (Magic: Protective mirror.)

Dagger: It goes far, straight, and repeatedly. (Magic: Sir Arthur's undefeatable double appears.)

Ghouls'n Ghosts is one big long maze. When you get to a certain play in the game, you can restart from there. Each stage has three places from which you can restart: the very beginning, the middle, and the end, which is helpful since the supermonster at the end is a challenge to kill.

Strategies

Hi's Hints

I like the treasures in this game. One is the pots that different characters carry around throughout the game. You'll find a variety of surprises in the pots. One big surprise is a baby. You capture the baby by running or jumping into it and get points. Weapons are also occasionally in the pots.

The chests are another interesting treasure. They can change you into different creatures with varying degrees of power. You can be turned temporarily into a duck, which has no power, or an old man with reduced powers. Occasionally, you'll get your armor back.

Statistically speaking, two out of the three things that happen are bad so you will usually get something bad. However, in some places chests always contain something nice. For instance, at the end of the swinging bridge section in Stage 2, the chests always contain armor or superarmor. As you go through the game, try the chest once or twice to find out whether it tends to contain good things or bad things and act accordingly.

When you're playing the game, try different routes through the screen. You can take a high road, jump across an obstruction, climb across the top of walls, or take a low road. If you try different approaches, you'll find that some routes are much easier to get through than others.

Patience is important in the game as well. Rarely will you die because the time ran out. Move quickly enough so villains don't come at you from the front as well as from the back, slowly enough to defeat all the enemies as you encounter them. If the time runs out, you need a new approach to killing the danger that confronts you. Try first one new approach and then another. Finding the right approach is really satisfying.

Tec's Tips

The basic objective of the game is this: each time you encounter a new type of creature, you have to figure out how to kill it. The game gives you three men and each man has up to two parts to his life. Since you start with armor, you can be hit and still be alive (but you're walking around in your underwear). Some hits or falls from high places can kill you.

To kill your enemies, you use six types of weapons. Some of them are better than others, but one of the weapons is the best one to have in at least one place in each one of the five phases. Part of the fun of the game is to figure out whether or not to capture a weapon when it's available.

Try each weapon both standing and kneeling. For instance, you come upon birds in the first level. When the birds are flying at you along the ground, you must kneel to kill them.

Using weapons is only one concern in this game. You must also learn to shoot overhead and jump over obstacles. There is often danger above you. You can jump over some of the danger on the ground. Don't forget that you can jump horizontally by pressing the D Button while you jump.

A big monster appears at the end of each stage. Each monster has a weakness. You can shoot forever and never kill the monster unless you hit its weak spot. For example, there's an armored monster with a green face at the end of Stage 1. You have to hit the green face many times to get the key that moves you on.

The monster at the end of Stage 4 is very difficult to kill. The worms and maggots do not kill the monster. The bases on the side of the monster from which the maggots come out must all be killed to obliterate the beast. It is extremely hard to do and impossible unless you shoot down. To shoot down, hold down the D Button, jump, and shoot while you're in the air. If you jump and shoot and jump and shoot, you can do it. Using this method coupled with and a great deal of patience, you can defeat the monster and get into Stage 5. The easiest way to kill the other monsters in Stage 4 is to kill them from below.

The best way to defeat the gatekeepers and worst monsters is to have a strategy, know their weak spots, and hit them many times.

Since the game is a process of trying different combinations of tactics on the different enemies, it is fun to play with someone else. Having two people with two control pads is a great way to pellet the enemy.

My last general strategy involves shooting. While you cannot move and shoot at the same time, there's no harm in shooting whenever you're standing still or in the air. Frequently, you'll kill an enemy that's just off the screen or that just came on the edge of the screen. Don't shoot all of the time because you can't make any progress. But whenever you can, it's a good idea to continue shooting. Many times you'll get lucky and defeat a particularly bad monster before it even comes onto the screen.

More Power Pointers

- There's a short period of time after your armor has been taken away when your naked image will shimmer. During this time, the enemy can't get you. Occasionally, you can get past them by using the fact that you're temporarily invincible. When you stop shimmering and become your regular, naked self, you're just as vulnerable as ever.

- Avoid the Bi-Fang (glob with big fangs). He won't attack you, but you will die if you touch him.

- Strike and strike again. Some monsters need several blows to get their attention and demise.

- You can select a level. After "Ghouls'n Ghosts" goes by on the title screen, press Up, Down, Left, and Right. Wait to hear music. Press A for half of Stage 1. Press Up and Start for half of Stage 2. Press Down and Start for Stage 3. Press Left and Start for Stage 4. Press Right and Start for Stage 5. Press Down, Right, and Start for Loki. Here is a super secret: Press A after any of the Stage 2 through Loki selections to start in the middle of a level.

Manufacturer Information

Company: Sega of America, Inc.

Address: P.O. Box 2167
          South San Francisco, CA
          94080

Game Counselor Hot Line: 415-871-GAME
(Please remember this is a regular toll charge telephone call.) 6 a.m. to 8:45 p.m. Pacific Time Monday through Friday and 8 a.m. to 5:45 p.m. Pacific Time Saturday and Sunday

Typical Price: $54.99

Golden Axe

Description

Death Adder has usurped Yuria and done the typical things that evil people do—hurt others and the way they live. He has invaded villages, killed many people, and taken the King and Princess along with the Golden Axe.

But there is good in this world. Three brave warriors are on the scene to defeat Death Adder. Ax-Battler is a strong man, Tyris-Flare is a magic-possessing woman who's quick with a sword, and Gilius-Thunderhead is a dwarf with speed and a nasty axe throw. Through these three, you'll be on an adventure to rescue the King, Princess, and Golden Axe.

Let's Play

The following buttons give you overall control of the game. Use them to control Ax-Battler, Tyris-Flare, and Gilius-Thunderhead.

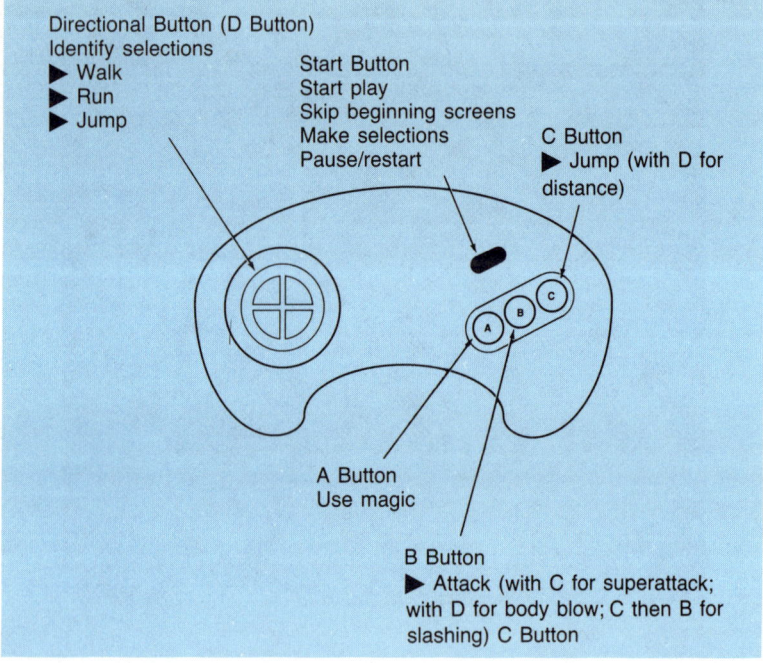

You can meander through a few screens to alter the game to your liking. First, select the mode of play:

- *Arcade:* It's a 5-day road trip you'll never forget because, by the time you've completed it, you'll know every bump in the road. When you press the Magic Button, you use all your magic.

- *Beginner:* This shorter version of Golden Axe ends at Stage 3. When you press the Magic Button, you use only two Magic Pots.

- *Duel:* Playing alone is a great way to practice fighting Death Adders soldiers. There are 12 duels. If you're playing with a partner, you can smash each other.

Golden Axe

You may also select Options to increase the number of your lives (called Credits), change the sound (press Start to preview), or switch the assignment of your buttons:

Button	Choice 1	Choice 2	Choice 3	Choice 4	Choice 5	Choice 6
A	Magic	Magic	Jump	Jump	Attack	Attack
B	Attack	Jump	Attack	Magic	Jump	Magic
C	Jump	Attack	Magic	Attack	Magic	Jump

A screen appears where you can pick which warrior you want to be. Tyris-Flare uses her Fire Magic; Gilius-Thunderhead may be short, but he can really somersault and use nasty Lightening Magic; and Ax-Battler has some wicked Volcano Magic.

Most players select the Arcade game. In it, there are eight stages:

- *Stage 1:* Woods where you can practice and get magic.

- *Stage 2:* Turtle Village where the villains are incredibly bad.

- *Stage 3:* Area between Turtle Island to the Mainland where there's a gaping crevasse to cross. You die if you make a mistake.

- *Stage 4:* Eagle Island, which is supposed to be on the back of a big eagle, where your opponents are tough. You'll have to cross some narrow bridges to test your maneuvering ability.

- *Stage 5:* Area between Eagle Island and the Palace (where the head of the Eagle is a good looking graphic). Once you arrive at the Palace, you must fight everybody again.

- *Stage 6:* Palace Gates where you meet Death Adder, Jr. He's not an innocent. He's got the power to do some nasty things with fire, and you've got to be good at avoiding his advances. The old adage, "like father, like son" is true here.

- *Stage 7:* Dungeon where the floor is scattered with holes and pits and all kinds of new trepidation. You must keep your wits and feet about you here.

- *Stage 8:* The Show Down where you see Death Adder and yearn for the days when you had only Jr. to deal with.

Watch your screen for valuable information. The top shows the number of Magic Pots you've gathered for superpower. At the bottom is the Hit Meter (the number of hits you have left before you lose a life) and the Life Counter (the number of lives you have left).

Strategies

Hi's Hints

The object of this game is to get as much magic and strength as you can. You get magic and strength by chasing and capturing the little elves. Catching them is tricky. But, watch carefully because they seem to follow the same pattern at the same place. As you learn the game, you can guess with some accuracy where they're going to run. The book that comes with the game says you're suppose to nudge them. I found that attacking them is more effective. Once they throw their magic pots, immediately run over and get the pot, or the elf will steal it back.

The elves also steal magic back when you're asleep. This typically seems to be at the end of a level. If this happens, get up as quickly as possible and start chasing them around.

While chasing the elves, remember that getting the strength bars are as important as the magic pots. When you get the strength, you get extra power levels, which make you better able to attack and work your magic. If you can boost your level of magic high enough, the magic can kill everybody. You won't have to kill a villain or use your magic twice to get out of a screen.

Magic is valuable so you must learn to save it. At first, it's easy to use it every time you get in trouble. Because parts of the game are very difficult to get past, you must save your magic for when there's two or three villains on the screen.

Also, magic isn't the solution to every problem. Using it doesn't necessarily kill everyone. For instance, you'll want to run right over to the female Amazon warriors after using magic and hack them once more. It takes that much to kill them.

One thing that annoys me about this game is the rating score at the end. You get a strength rating and a score from A to F. The scoring can be discouraging.

Tec's Tips

Develop a strategy to determine how and when to attack and when to run. You have to kill all the villains on a screen. The game doesn't let you run away and leave any behind.

I attack everyone in the back. If I can run and jump over them, I do that. When I attack, I find the weakest spots in the back. In the same vein, I pay particular attention to protecting my back. I always face the villains because one blow to the back is death. The worst thing you can do is to stand where villains can surround you. If they get you on both sides, they can take your energy, and you won't be able to defend yourself.

I often jump on the Bizarrian critters, ride around, and attack from there. You can hit the villains, and it is harder for them to hit back. Riding on the critters keeps the enemy away and lets you attack them. If you can get them up against the wall or edge of the screen, you'll have an advantage because they have fewer directions in which they can attack and kill you.

Some of the villains have to be hit more than once, and some are dead after a single blow. An effective strategy is to jump and attack. It takes quite a bit of practice to be good. You have to see what the villain is doing with his weapon and then stick your weapon in the weak spot. Overall, jumping seems to give a better angle for attack.

When using the Attack Button, I hold the controller with my hand over the top on that side because I want to hit it repeatedly. The more times I hit it quickly, the better able I am to work magic.

Use several jumps in a row to get in a good position. If you can get the high ground on the screen, that will help because your enemies are vulnerable while they're jumping. You can swipe at them several times with your attack blows when they jump up to get you.

If you're in a high place, you can pick the time when you want to jump down for the attack. A combination of jumping and hitting the Attack Button several times is a very good fighting skill. If you stay on the ground you're going to get killed. If you're in the air, you're in a less vulnerable position.

You can't just march in and attack somebody any time it strikes your fancy. If a villain is in a frenzy and swinging a weapon, wait until it becomes less active. In fact, many of the villains in this game become less violent if you wait for them to calm down. Once they've settled down, run in close and repeatedly press the Attack Button. Or jump over to where they are and press your Attack Button repeatedly. Another method is to jump over the villain's head, twirl around, and then hit. (Use the B and C Buttons together to twirl.) Just make sure you land facing your opponent. Don't jump, twirl, and stop with your back exposed.

Hi and I play Golden Axe together. In a one-player game, it is hard to get behind a villain to deal a death blow. With two players, it's easy because you can't get surrounded unless you get together. The villain has to attack one of you and expose it's back to the other. If it's back is exposed to you, you can go in for the kill. Also, if you don't stay apart, you can accidently strike your partner. We have some special plays. For example, I'll run near somebody but not too close. In that way, I expose the villain's back to Hi and she takes over. Two players can also kill more quickly those villains that must be attacked repeatedly.

More Power Pointers

- When you approach a bridge or need to jump, run right up to the last moment and jump. But be aware that it's easy to fall off the edges. For example, when you jump across the gaps in Stage 3 (crossing from Turtle Island to the Mainland), you can think you're standing on the edge, go too far, and fall off.

- Stage 4 has narrow bridges where you need to stay well in the safe path. The edge can be deadly.

- Press the Attack Button repeatedly for different actions. For example, if you press it three times, you may toss the villain down and spin him. Other options are to hack or poke your handle at the villain.

Manufacturer Information

Company: Sega of America, Inc.

Address: P.O. Box 2167
South San Francisco, CA
94080

Game Counselor Hot Line: 415-871-GAME
(Please remember this is a regular toll charge telephone call.) 6 a.m. to 8:45 p.m. Pacific Time Monday through Friday and 8 a.m. to 5:45 p.m. Pacific Time Saturday and Sunday

Typical Price: $59.99

Last Battle

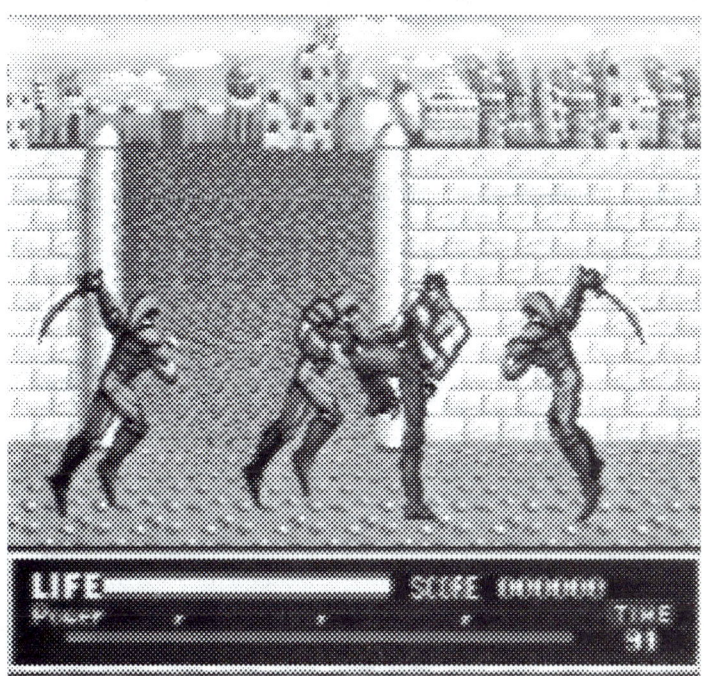

Description

Last Battle is the result of a long history of clashes—lost motherlands, periods of peace, prodigal sons, and good versus evil. The essence of today's situation is that the martial art of jet-kwon-do will help you in the last battle against Garokk. You, as Aarzak, are out to save Alyssa and the world. It's a common theme but a very uncommon last battle.

Let's Play

The following buttons give you overall control of the game. Use them to control Aarzak.

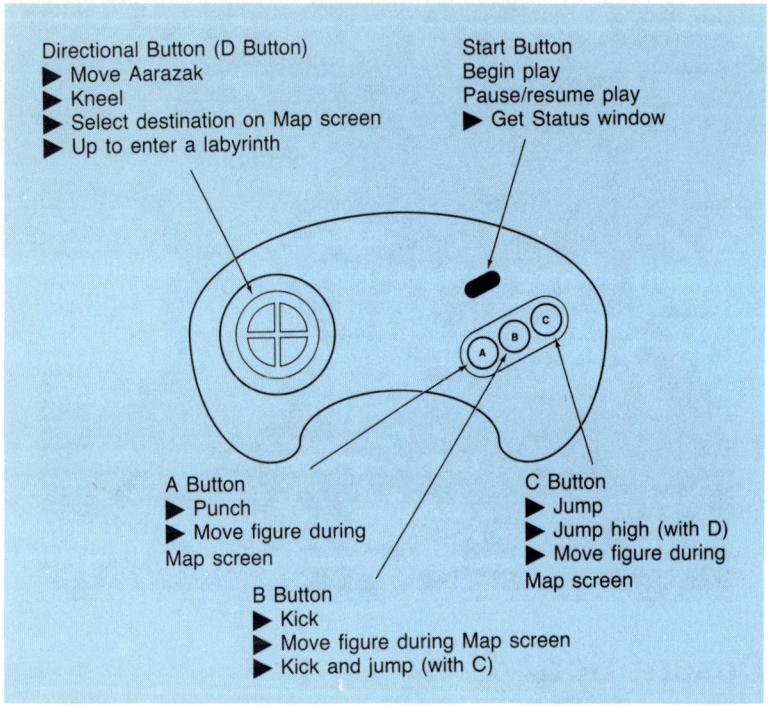

Last Battle has four chapters with each chapter sporting seven to ten areas.

- *Chapter 1: New Legend Creators* with the following areas: 1) Western, 2) Wilderness, 3) Hulk's, 4) Prison, 5) Quiet Village, 6) Rebel's Prison, 7) Southern, 8) Butcher's, 9) Eternal Plain

- *Chapter 2: Golden Assassins* with the following areas: 1) First Gate, 2) Second Gate, 3) Third Gate, 4) Quiet Village, 5) Fourth Gate, 6) Forbidden City, 7) Seashore

- *Chapter 3: Ultimate Hell* with the following areas: 1) Pirate Ship 1, 2) Pirate Ship 2, 3) Savage Land 1, 4) Savage Land 2, 5) Eternal Plain, 6) Dry River Bed, 7) Western Village, 8) Desert, 9) The Gromm Castle

- *Chapter 4: The Destroyer's Fate* with the following areas: 1) Valley of No Return, 2) Castle Entrance, 3) Great Coliseum, 4) The Garokk Castle, 5) Eternal Plain, 6) The Village, 7) East Mausoleum, 8) West Mausoleum, 9) Northern Village, 10) Tombstone

This game comes with a map so you can better find your way around. The map is a great help! After you get through an area, the Map screen pops up. Use the D Button to point out the direction to go then press the A, B, or C Button to move on.

Another useful feature is the Status window. It shows you Aarzak's life, power, and score (the left number is actual and the right number is potential). When you're hit and the power is high, you lose less life. When you're hit at a lower power level, you lose more life.

The bottom of the screen reviews Aarzak's existence via the Life Guage Score, Power Guage, and Time. When time runs out, you still have some life, but your power diminishes considerably. To get more power, defeat bullies. At the end of each chapter, you completely lose your power, so take chances and enjoy yourself.

Each chapter has a labyrinth, but you must have enough power and points to enter it. You can't get out unless you find a friend who knows the lay of the labyrinth. Friends and enemies can talk to you along the way.

Strategies

 ### Hi's Hints

Last Battle is a maze game where you kick and kill. However, you do meet some nice people along the way.

Time does play a role in each area, but it is not a major issue. In a labyrinth, time stands still so take it easy.

My major strategy is to avoid getting hit. This game does not pass out a generous amount of life. You must save every bit of it. The game gets easier as you go farther because you're level of power increases. When your power increases, you life decreases at a slower rate. It's essential that you guard your life at the beginning and attack and kill every enemy to boost your power level.

Also, once you know where the labyrinth is in a given chapter, wait until your life energy is running low (and you've made a few kills) before entering the labyrinth. That way, you use the energy you had before you entered, and you get your energy back when you leave.

Tec's Tips

When it comes to defense, punching works at the beginning, kicking works next, and ducking and kicking works after that. Jumping and striking is a good strategy when your enemies are sitting on a wall. Just jump up and punch or jump up and kick.

Press the B and C Buttons together for a double kick. A fancy approach is to jump in the air with B and C Buttons simultaneously and to wiggle the D Button. This technique lets you kick both ways while you're in the air. I use this when I'm surrounded. It kills a number of people in a hurry.

Strike quickly. When you see someone on the screen, throw a punch right away. It typically takes villains some

Last Battle

time to set up before they hit you so take advantage of that small amount of time. Another benefit of killing the villains before they kill you is that your power level goes up. As your power level increases, it reaches white tick marks on the bar at the bottom of the screen and you get more power. When that happens, you visibly bulk up.

Ducking is more defensive than it is aggressive (although ducking and kicking seems to work pretty well). Items that you will want to duck fly through the air. When villains come from above, duck and strike. Otherwise, they might get you.

Also, don't expose your back to your enemies. They have no ethics about where they strike.

Your enemies are relatively easy to defeat. The boss guys are among the exceptions.

Not all villains look like people. For example, there are rolling rocks and swords that shoot. Kick those just like you would anything else, or they will take your life force.

In this game, it's difficult to advance if you don't kill everything on the screen. You very definitely want to go into the rooms inside the labyrinth because that's where you get your life back up. This game doesn't let you start where you left off. You have to conserve your life and go into the labyrinth in each level to advance. Also, your strength increases at the end of some of the screens simply because you have progressed that far.

You need to develop a strategy and figure out the order in which you want to do things since some of the levels are much easier than others. Explore the maze as you plot your next move.

Often villains lurk overhead and then fall on you or shoot at you. However, if you are observant, you can see a small piece of them before they attack. For instance, swords fall from the roof in the labyrinth in Chapter 1. If you pay attention, you can see the tips of the swords in enough time to deal with them.

You cannot jump very far; you can't jump over holes in mazes. However, when you're on top of an object, you may want to jump up because you'll find secret overhead passages that you wouldn't otherwise be able to find.

More Power Pointers

- Rough out your own map and jot locations on it to remember important spots.
- When your power is low, go to easy areas to kill villains and recharge your power level. When your power level is high, tackle the more difficult areas.
- When the villains have swords, ducking and striking or ducking and kicking is effective.
- Always read the conversations for clues.
- You can select up to a chapter. When you reach the end of play, hold down the A, B, and C Buttons while you press Start four times.

Manufacturer Information

Company: Sega of America, Inc.

Address: P.O. Box 2167
South San Francisco, CA
94080

Game Counselor Hot Line: 415-871-GAME
(Please remember this is a regular toll charge telephone call.) 6 a.m. to 8:45 p.m. Pacific Time Monday through Friday and 8 a.m. to 5:45 p.m. Pacific Time Saturday and Sunday

Typical Price: $49.99

Rambo III

Description

Rambo is off to rescue Colonel Trautman, his old friend from the long nights and days in Vietnam. Learning that Trautman was captured as he tried to cross the Afghanistan border, Rambo sets out to deliver Trautman from his captors.

Amid bombs, grenades, and machine gun splatter, you are there as Rambo. Only you can rescue Trautman and return him to safety with both of you alive.

Let's Play

The following buttons give you overall control of the game. Use them to control Rambo's work.

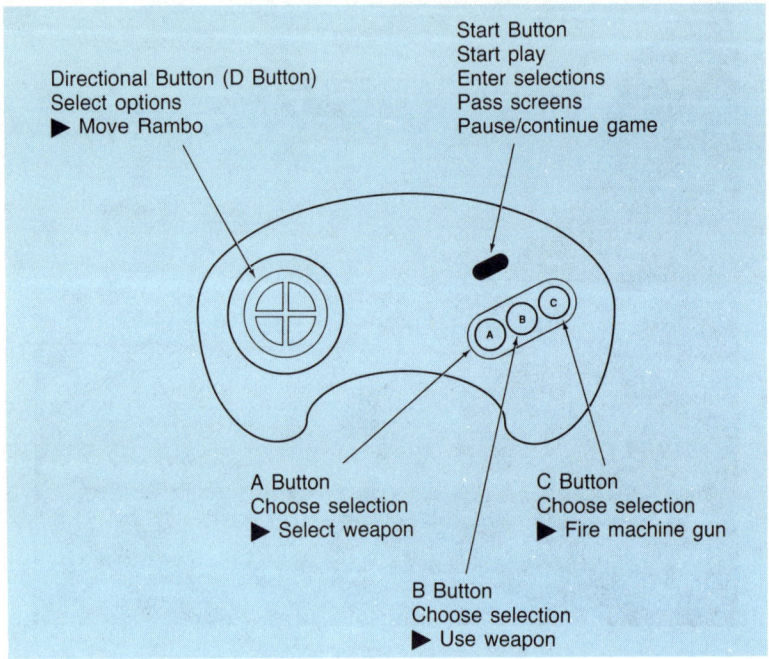

Directional Button (D Button)
Select options
▶ Move Rambo

Start Button
Start play
Enter selections
Pass screens
Pause/continue game

A Button
Choose selection
▶ Select weapon

C Button
Choose selection
▶ Fire machine gun

B Button
Choose selection
▶ Use weapon

Like most Sega games, you can set up certain options for play. Select Options after the title screen. On the Options screen, you may select:

- Difficulty (1 is the easiest and 4 is the hardest)
- The number of lives Rambo has (1 to 5)
- The action of the A, B, and C Buttons (SEL selects special weapons, SPE fires special weapons, and MAC produces machine gun fire)

The sound test on the Options screen allows you to select from sounds 1 through 11. Select Exit and press the A, B, or C Button to play.

Rambo III

Your weaponry appears on the left of the screen along with the number of weapons remaining. You start with a fairly hefty cache including a machine gun, knife, bow and arrow, explosives, and time bombs. The number of remaining lives and the number of the round appear in the lower right screen.

The machine gun with an infinite number of bullets is your trustiest weapon. If you fire from a stationary position, the bullets will spray. If you fire while running, the bullets will go straight. Hold down the button for continuous fire. To attack with any other weapon, select it then press the button to use it. Hold down the bow and arrow button for a more powerful explosion. But don't hold it down too long or you may be dead before you can shoot. The time bomb will always go off in 5 seconds.

There are six missions in Rambo III. A bonus skirmish occurs after Missions 1, 3, 5, and 6. Bows and arrows kill Hind helicopters and T2-A tanks.

These are the six missions whether you choose to accept them or not.

- *Mission 1:* Within the perimeter of the enemy camp, you blast and blow up everything.

- *Mission 2:* In the underground prison, shoot at each prisoner until he identifies himself. When you find the secret agent, get out of there fast.

- *Mission 3:* Get into the heavily guarded enemy arsenal through the gate.

- *Mission 4:* Complete destruction of the enemy arsenal is your goal.

- *Mission 5:* In the heliport, use bows and arrows to shoot tanks but be alert for the troops when they come and mow them down with machine gun fire. Exit is the way out.

- *Mission 6:* Find Colonel Trautman. When you have rescued him, your mission is a success!

Annihilating the enemy gives you points. Soldiers are worth more points in later missions. Trucks (500 points), jeeps (800 points), and tanks (1,000 points) are the same value throughout the game. The more helicopters you shoot down in a row, the more points you get.

Strategies

Hi's Hints

If you are new to this game, give yourself five lives. Use the Options screen to set this up.

I watch for those extra lives and weapons. A smiling face is an extra life, an A in a box is a bow and arrow, and a B in a box is a time bomb. Get them if at all possible. Knifing some soldiers also gives you extra lives. Tec can do it, but I have a hard time with it. It's easier for me to kill a soldier with a machine gun from 20 paces than to sneak up and knife him.

As you move, pay attention to bullets. They show up on the screen, and I try to stay out of their way. Bullets have a limited range. Run away and the bullets probably won't reach you.

When I get killed, I try to use it to my advantage. Being killed makes you temporarily invincible. This is the time to get set up to blow the enemies away. This can be helpful when you must defend yourself against attack on all sides. The Pause Button is also very useful when you're suddenly surrounded by several potentially dangerous situations. I pause and figure out how to escape. Once I restart, however, I have to be ready to go.

I've noticed that if you continue a game, you don't get all your resources refreshed. You can use your knife and machine gun as often as you want, but there's a limited number of bows and arrows and bombs.

If you're running from a soldier and have a number of bombs, drop one. The solder might get killed.

Tec's Tips

Be careful when using special weapons. If you don't have many, save them and choose carefully where you use them. When you drop a bomb, run away, or it will blow you up, too. When you encounter a particularly deadly target, use more than one bomb. Drop two or three and get out of the area. There are some things you just can't accomplish any other way. For example, to get to the end of Mission 3 with bombs in tow, turn right at the green sheds, or you won't get through the gate.

On the whole, in the normal round, bombs are the most effective weapon. They can get you through a gate or a tower. You can get them easily from the watch towers so you won't run out of them as often as you will the bows and arrows. The bows and arrows are good for trucks.

Before you start, select the weapon you'll need to save time flipping between weapons. As you get to know the missions, you'll know when to set up for the weapon you need.

Practice with the bow and arrow because that's what you'll use at bonus battle time. Move out, aim, get maximum power, and fire so you can get on to the next mission. There's a bonus for time. The faster you do the bonus round, the more points you'll get. If you get killed in the bonus battle, that's it. You have to destroy the enemy in that battle to go on to the next mission. You'll need a strategy. For example, at the end of Mission 1, you come up against the helicopter. It's important to use shelter. Hide behind rocks, or the enemy will kill you. Get the arrow to the highest power, aim, and shoot.

Once you find a prisoner in a mission, you must fight your way to the exit. It's important that you find an exit once you have a prisoner. You might want to find the exit before you look for the prisoner. That way, you can exit quickly.

Sneaking up and knifing a soldier is a good skill to have. You probably don't want to use it in Mission 1 because there is so much going on. But starting in Mission 3 where the enemy is camouflaged (and possibly in Mission 2 if you aren't quite as agressive), it's worth the risk to sneak up and kill them. This is particularly true when you don't have many bows and arrows and bombs because you not only get points but you also get extra bows and arrows and bombs.

When you run out of resources, play to increase the number of bombs and bows and arrows available to you. Knife somebody (the camouflaged people are the least risky). Go ahead and be risky, die if you must, and then use the Continue feature. When you die, you keep your resources. This is one way to create a stockpile of bows and arrows and bombs, which makes a run at the end of the mission easier since you're fully equipped. For example, in about 10 minutes I recently played three games and accumulated over 40 bows and arrows and 40 bombs. When the enemy killed me, I just said "Yes, I'd like to continue" and got out of the mission with more resources.

Always have a strategy. For example, to get out of the starting place in Mission 4, you must blow up a piece of wall. You need quite a few bombs to get out. Also in Mission 4, pieces of the wall open up like doorways. They're easy to find. You have to blow up the gold-colored pieces of the wall to get through.

By the way, the hit ratio is a misnomer. It's not a ratio of anything divided by anything else. Each time you kill something inside the arsenal, you get 4% until it adds to 100%. The exit is in the upper left corner. This area is a problem since it seems to be a gathering place for both people and helicopters. You'd be well advised to wait until you have a hit ratio of about 86% so that when you kill off the helicopters, you can exit.

More Power Pointers

- When you see Continue Game, select Yes to keep the weapons you had at the end.
- You can never have more than 99 bows and arrows or 99 bombs.
- If you hold the Fire Button down, the machine gun will fire forever.
- Any time you get by the railroad tracks, you're looking for trouble. Do the right and upper right sides of the maze first.
- Running on the diagonal and shooting while you run will help you to kill more people.
- Don't bump into the enemies. If you touch them, you're dead. They don't have to shoot you.

Manufacturer Information

Company: Sega of America, Inc.

Address: P.O. Box 2167
South San Francisco, CA
94080

Game Counselor Hot Line: 415-871-GAME
(Please remember this is a regular toll charge telephone call.) 6 a.m. to 8:45 p.m. Pacific Time Monday through Friday and 8 a.m. to 5:45 p.m. Pacific Time Saturday and Sunday

Suggested List Price: $49.99

Super Hang-On

Description

With Super Hang On, you can have the simple fun of racing a motorcycle in an easy race. Or you can take on the thrilling challenge of fast-paced racing with not only your skill as a variable but also that of your opponents and sponsors. You choose the level of play. This is bike racing as real as any game gets.

At any level of play, your first and foremost adversary is the clock. From there, who or what you compete against depends on which of the game versions you've taken on. In the Arcade game, your mechanic and sponsor are primarily on your side when you falter. In the

Genesis game called the Original game, life on the bike is motorcycle mania at its best. There's a whole lot more going on.

Let's Play

The following buttons give you overall control of the game. Use them to control your motorcycle from start to finish (or crash).

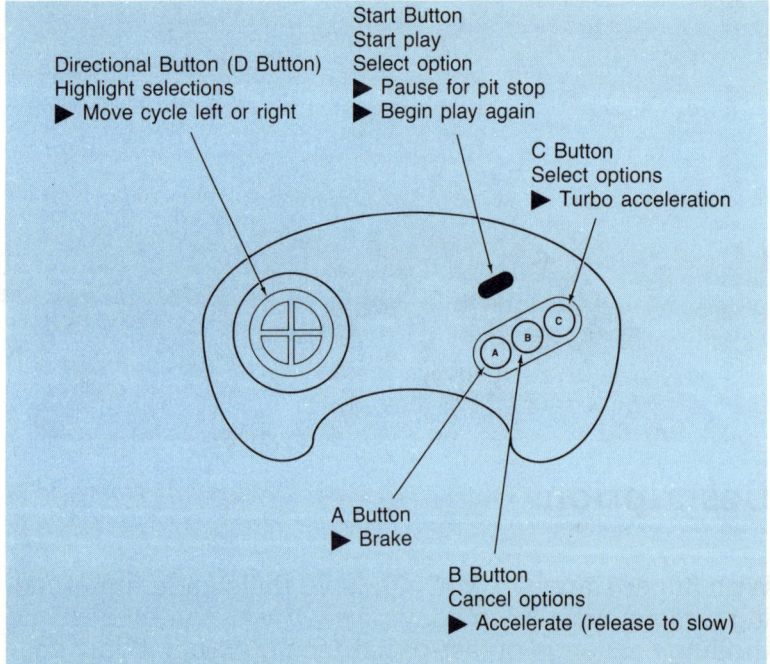

Directional Button (D Button)
Highlight selections
▶ Move cycle left or right

Start Button
Start play
Select option
▶ Pause for pit stop
▶ Begin play again

C Button
Select options
▶ Turbo acceleration

A Button
▶ Brake

B Button
Cancel options
▶ Accelerate (release to slow)

At the title screen, press Start. Use the D Button to select New Game or Password then press Start or the C Button.

Passwords can trip you up if you're not informed. Super Hang On will give you a password if you finish a race. Use Sega's supplied password to use the same machine you raced with in the last game. To use the

Super Hang-On

password, press the D Button to select a letter on the Password screen and press the C Button to enter the letter. Or, if you goof, select the letter and press the A Button to "de-enter" it.

Several screens appear after you select New Game. Use the D Button to identify a selection then press the C Button to choose. (Think of C for Choose.) These are the types of selections you'll be able to make.

- Choose either Arcade mode (a simpler race) or Genesis Original mode (with more variables to control).

- If you selected Arcade mode, identify the difficulty. Africa/Beginner has 6 stages of play, Asia/Junior has 10 stages of play, America/Senior has 14 stages, and Europe/Expert has a whopping 16 stages of play. From Africa to Europe the number of curves, traffic, and obstacles increases.

- If you picked Original mode, more variables come into play. You can command the parts you buy and the mechanic you hire. Also from the Command area, select Race to start the music and race or End to stop the race and resume later. When you enter the Original mode, you meet your mechanic and sponsor. You also see and hear from your rival. All are healthy competitors. The lap times, wins, and losses are shown.

- Pick from some interesting background music. This is your last moment to relax before the race. After you select the music (or let Sega choose it for you), get the feel of those handle bars. The race will start soon.

- Put your initials on the leader board. If you place seventh or better, select your initials with the D and C Button. Then select ED and press the C Button to play again.

Strategies

Hi's Hints

I think its fun to play in Arcade mode. Go as fast as you can. The B Button gives pretty good speed. It's quick, but you should be able to deal with it.

Anticipate what's coming down the track. It isn't as complicated as it looks. Pay special attention to curves; they are usually marked in the beginner course. In really tight curves, you can do two things. You could brake (use the A Button), but braking takes too much time. You could also lean into the curve and try to cut in close. If you release the speed button (B Button), the bike straightens up. You don't have to brake, just let up on the B Button when you lean too much.

I don't worry about skidding. There's no way to lay the bike down. Just hold on and keep up the speed.

I like to hold the B Button down almost all the time. I don't get into too much trouble if I do. Turbo mode gives you superfast acceleration. You save time, but you also get into trouble by smashing into obstacles. I don't use it much.

When it comes to obstacles, I often go around them. The lower levels don't usually have a severe time penalty for getting off the course and going around a sign or tree before getting back on the track.

When a rider is in front of me, I've found that continuing what I'm doing and trying to ride around doesn't work well. What does work is to give the rider a jiggle (with the D Button); the rider tends to move out of the way. My sidekick, Tec, likes to hit the turbo button when he has a good angle on the motorcycle rider to scoot past him quickly.

The best thing about this game is that I can complete a stage and get on the leader board rather quickly.

Super Hang-On

Tec's Tips

Super Hang On is a super game. When the race starts, I have my fingers on both the B and C Buttons for maximum acceleration. At the first turn, I pull off the C Button and spend more time with the B Button, reserving the C Button to shoot around other riders or blast down a straightaway. Unfortunately the more advanced levels have fewer straightaways so high speeds are difficult to maintain.

For cornering I usually back off of the B Button, but I also find that tapping on the C Button on an inside curve can dramatically improve my time.

Never hold the D Button down for long. Either tap it or hold it for short periods of time as if you are on a motorcycle and yank on the throttle to boost the speed.

I keep one eye on my bike, one on what's coming up, and another on the time. I know that's three eyes, but you need them all. When the time is running out in a stage, I hit the Turbo button and go as fast as I can. Checkpoints for extended play appear along the straight-away. So when there are 5 seconds to go, pull out the stops and go for it. There's almost always a gate over the next hill.

Don't tangle with other riders. Pass them or catch them on a curve, but don't touch them. The game will tip you over in the wrong direction, and this will slow you down.

I often play the Genesis Original mode. I like the variety and challenge. I get more messages on the screen about my bike and how it's behaving. When I have money, I spend it on my engine. I had to shake a few bad habits after playing the Arcade mode. In the Arcade game, there's no harm in spinning out on the turns (in fact, it's fun). But, in the Original mode, that kind of driving wears out your tires.

You have to accumulate a number of wins to get a new sponsor, but having a better sponsor makes a real difference in your performance and victories.

Don't underestimate the women in this game. As drivers, mechanics, and sponsors, they can hold their own with the men.

More Power Pointers

- Don't crash! There is a time penalty associated with setting up the bike and getting it on the course. This makes it difficult. Except in early and beginning levels, the time penalty makes getting into an extended play difficult. If you want to go anywhere in this game, think of safety first. Of course, if you do crash, just press Start (there are no trips to the hospital or morgue in this game).

- The most important information at the top of the race screen is Time. When it hits zero, the race is over. The next most important information is the S(tart) to G(oal) graph. It shows your position on the overall course. If you have the time and you're not near the goal, live dangerously. If you're close to the goal with just a little time, do as the name of the game suggests—hang on. The screen also shows the Top score, your Score and Speed, as well as the Course and Stage of the race.

- The score is less important in the Arcade mode than in the Genesis Original mode. In the Arcade version, the score gets you on the leader board, and time is the factor in finishing the race. With the Genesis Original version, the score gives you money, which can have a large affect on the outcome of the race. With the money, you can get better hired hands and better parts for your bike and become a better competitor (maybe you went to a riding class or something).

- Checkpoint arches take you to the next stage. Time from the last stage isn't lost when you go to a new stage. So speed is always important.

- In the Genesis Original mode, you want to spend money to improve your game. Generally, the more expensive frames are better; the Titanium Monocoque Frame is the best. The same is true with engines, brakes, mufflers, oil, tires, and mechanics. New sponsors come along when you get five wins more than the rival.

Manufacturer Information

Company: Sega of America, Inc.

Address: P.O. Box 2167
South San Francisco, CA
94080

Game Counselor Hot Line: 415-871-GAME
(Please remember this is a regular toll charge telephone call.) 6 a.m. to 8:45 p.m. Pacific Time Monday through Friday and 8 a.m. to 5:45 p.m. Pacific Time Saturday and Sunday

Typical Price: $49.99

The Revenge of Shinobi

Description

Shinobi is back with ninja powers of unfathomed dimensions. Through study, practice, and meditation, you have learned the ways of ninja magic. As Musashi, the master ninja, you are a sure weapon. The enemy, Neo Zeed, is a world cancer having already taken over eight districts. The Neo Zeed come in many forms. Their reason for being is to take over the entire world. Use your powers to find them and destroy them so the world may again be safe.

Let's Play

The following buttons give you overall control of the game. Use them to control the activity of Musashi.

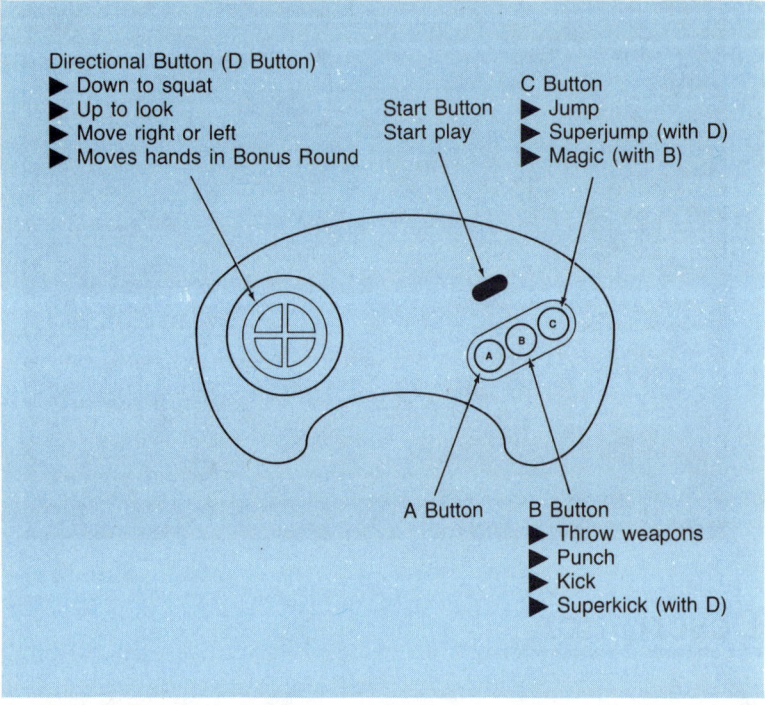

Directional Button (D Button)
▶ Down to squat
▶ Up to look
▶ Move right or left
▶ Moves hands in Bonus Round

Start Button
Start play

C Button
▶ Jump
▶ Superjump (with D)
▶ Magic (with B)

A Button

B Button
▶ Throw weapons
▶ Punch
▶ Kick
▶ Superkick (with D)

The Options screen allows you to choose the sound, the level (controls both difficulty and number of lives), and the number of Shurikins (throwing knives) Musashi carries. You may also set the control pad differently:

- *Type 1:* A Ninjitsu, B Attack, C Jump
- *Type 2:* A Attack, B Jump, C Ninjitsu
- *Type 3:* A Jump, B Attack, C Ninjitsu
- *Type 4:* A Ninjitsu, B Jump, C Attack

Select Exit and press Start to begin seeking out the Neo Zeed. As you begin, watch your life bar. When you have worn yourself out, you die. Increase your life with a score of 50,000 and 100,000 and also by finishing a scene.

Crates contain valuable weapons. A superweapon is the Power Pack. It makes you stronger, and you gain a sword and the Cross Guard skill to shield you from enemy Death Stars. Crates may also contain more Shurikins, a small heart (for two life bars), the Musashi (for an extra life), Ninjitsu (for magic), and a time bomb. There are also hidden weapons to watch for.

When you're really in a difficult position, press the Start Button to select ninja magic. Select from four jitsus (secret arts) then press the Start Button again. The secret arts are:

- *Ikazuchi, the Art of Thunder:* It surrounds you with protection.

- *Kariu, the Art of the Fire Dragon:* It is a protective and burning fire column.

- *Fushin, the Art of Floating:* It gives you enhanced jumping power.

- *Mijin, the Art of Pulverizing:* With it, you become a human explosion and lose a life to destroy everything on the screen.

The Neo Zeed have overtaken the following districts:

- *District 1:* Ibaraki Province, Japan with scenes in the Bamboo Garden and the House of Confusion, as well as an escape route.

- *District 2:* Tokyo with scenes at the Waterfall, the Backstreet, and the Bistro.

- *District 3:* The Military Base with scenes at the Airport Compound, the Cargo Jet, and the Computer Vault.

- *District 4:* Detroit with scenes from the Junkyard, the Motor Mill, and the Side Yard.

- *District 5:* Area Code 818 with scenes from the Laser 'Scraper, the Freeway, and the High Speed Chase.

- *District 6:* Chinatown with scenes from the Kung Fu Gang, the Train, and Spiderman.
- *District 7:* New York with scenes from the Breakwater, the Machine Room, and the Cargo Hold.
- *District 8:* Neo Zeed Marine Stronghold with scenes from the Searchlight, the Cellar Maze, and the Inner Sanctum.

It is a hard, long journey. But, as a ninja you have prepared all your life for what awaits. Be like a snake and slip through the breaks in the wall and strike when you must.

Strategies

Hi's Hints

To start, I usually go into the Options screen and get some knives, which will make the game easy. At the easy level, you get quite a few lives per game, and, of course, it's a lot easier to advance.

You can set the controls so that the different types of martial arts are on the different A, B, and C Buttons. But, since I'm used to many other Genesis games, I use type 1 (which is the way it is if you don't change it). This puts the jump on the C Button, which is the button that the jump is on when playing most other games.

When playing, you can pause whenever necessary in the middle of the game to select the type of secret art to use at that point. I need this feature only when I get in too much trouble. I can usually kill most of the villains by simply attacking, but when I can't successfully attack, I press Pause. It doesn't hurt me, and, furthermore, I can look at what's going on and figure out the best secret art solution. For instance, if my life bar is really low, I can destroy everything on the screen at the expense of only the remaining life bar by using the Mijin, which makes a big explosion that destroys everything on the screen. If, on the other hand, I have a larger life bar left, I can get some temporary protection when I'm in trouble by using the Ikazuchi (the Art of Thunder). I'm protected, I don't get injured, my life bar doesn't decrease, and it gives me some more time.

Always keep an eye on how much life you have left. When you're getting low, you should invoke a Ninjitsu. You have nothing to lose, and it will save you time and energy and move you on through the screen.

This isn't my favorite game since it is basically a slaughter game where I, with righteousness on my side, am out to revenge a death.

Tec's Tips

If you've played Shinobi on the Master System, you basically know how to play this game. The Revenge of Shinobi has just improved Shinobi.

The crates are good to go after. Almost all of them give you more knives, increase your life, or give you an extra life. There is a bomb that comes up from time to time to hurt you. But you can usually get away from the blast.

The same crate in the same location in the same level almost always has the same thing in it. Occasionally, there's a surprise. But for the most part, you can figure out the good crates from the bad ones. If you know where the bombs are, don't kick the crates open. Jump over them and keep going. By the way, the crates in the most out of the way or most defended places tend to contain the extra lives and secret powers.

This is a game of discovery. You have to find the weak spots. For instance, you can't kill the swordsmen from the front. You have to jump over them and kill them from behind in just one blow. Each of the villans has a weakness—some are easy, and some are challenging. With some, you have to both jump and shoot, often repeatedly.

69

Jumping and ducking to avoid and shoot the enemy are very important parts of the game. Jump extra high by hitting the jump button twice then flip. If you do this and shoot your weapons, you lay a spray of knives out.

Follow the red-orange arrows that lead you to the way out of the particular level. There are dead ends. You're welcome to enter them and fight valiant battles against villains that don't make any difference in terms of getting through the level and saving your life. I don't bother with them.

Ninjitsu magics are important. One of my favorite techniques is to use the Fushin magic (the Art of Floating) at the beginning of every game. It makes my jumping more accurate, I can jump higher and get better distance. This is especially helpful in the mazes when I have to get to upper levels. The best thing is that this power stays with me until the scene ends even when I pick up another one of the magics.

If you're coming upon a section of the game that you have had trouble getting through, try the Art of the Fire Dragon (the Kariu). It doesn't just deal with what's on the screen, it lasts a reasonable amount of time, and you innocently massacre everything in your way with fire.

It is possible to get some extra ninjitsu in the same life. You get to use only the Art of Floating and one other jitsu in one life. The crates occasionally have others. You've got to get them to go far in the game.

More Power Pointers

- If you are standing near the enemy and attack, you'll stab him. If you are crouching near the enemy and attack, you'll kick. If there is no enemy close, the attack results in a sling of Shurikins. If you attack during a jump and somersault, eight Shurikins go off.

- Go and exit arrows will keep you headed toward your destination.
- Choose your battles according to the most points you may receive.

Manufacturer Information

Company: Sega of America, Inc.

Address: P.O. Box 2167
South San Francisco, CA
94080

Game Counselor Hot Line: 415-871-GAME
(Please remember this is a regular toll charge telephone call.) 6 a.m. to 8:45 p.m. Pacific Time Monday through Friday and 8 a.m. to 5:45 p.m. Pacific Time Saturday and Sunday

Typical Price: $59.99

Thunder Force II

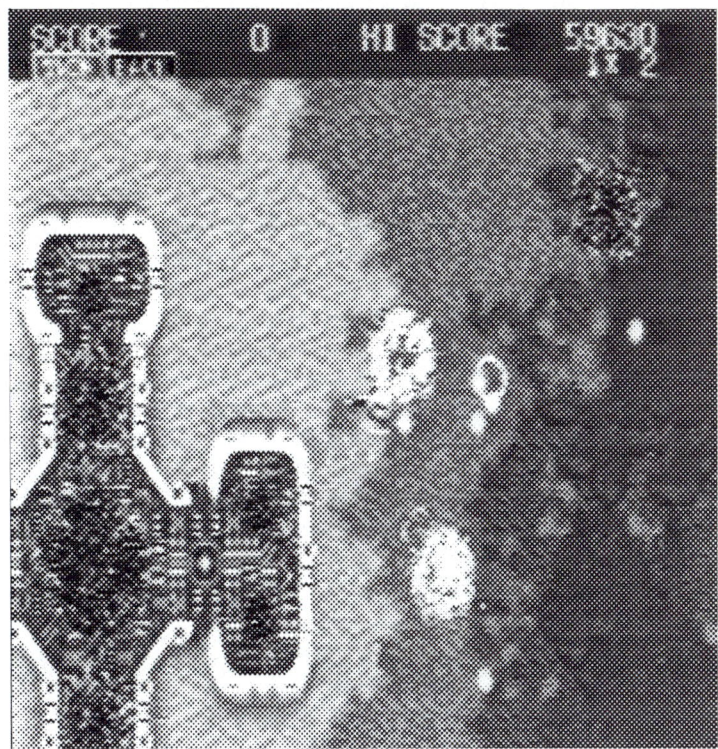

Description

Flying high above the Planet Nebula, the mind cannot imagine the danger that lurks ahead. Yours is a difficult mission. Do not underestimate what you are about to undertake. The terrorist Lone Star System has shattered a brief period of peace for Planet Nebula. Your mission is to maneuver the spaceship Thunder Force II to the final destination: the port below Nebula's surface where the mother ship, Plealos, is docked.

This is no Sunday drive or picnic in the park. The inhabitants of the Lone Star System are without conscience, and the path to Plealos is deadly. Get all the weapons you can and employ them well. Save the planet; save the people.

Let's Play

The following buttons give you overall control of the game. Use them to control the ship, Thunder Force II.

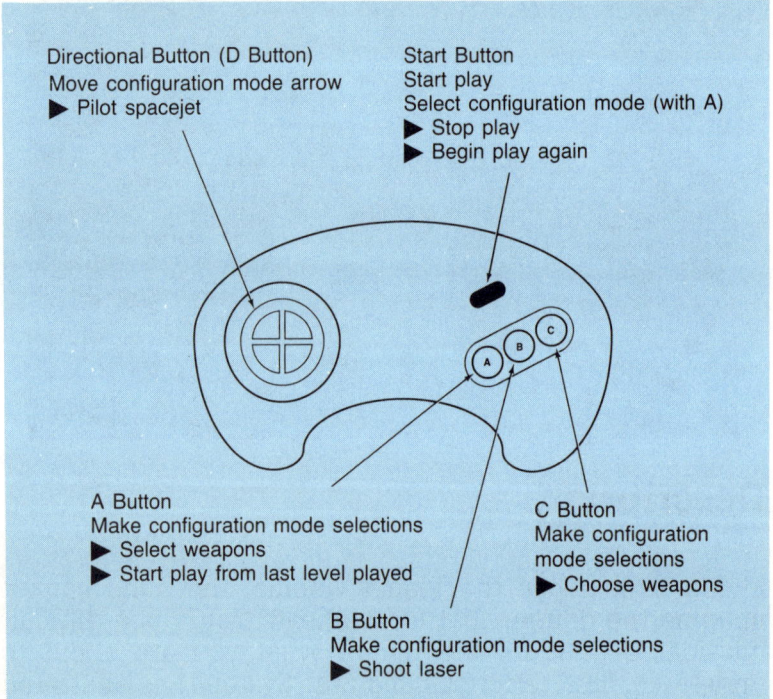

Directional Button (D Button)
Move configuration mode arrow
▶ Pilot spacejet

Start Button
Start play
Select configuration mode (with A)
▶ Stop play
▶ Begin play again

A Button
Make configuration mode selections
▶ Select weapons
▶ Start play from last level played

B Button
Make configuration mode selections
▶ Shoot laser

C Button
Make configuration mode selections
▶ Choose weapons

First, get behind the controls of your space jet. At the title screen, press the Start Button. You can press Start to begin play. Or you can press the A Button and the Start Button at the same time to go to the Configuration Mode screen. The options here are:

- *Difficulty:* If you are in Training, you can begin only at the first level. If you are Normal, you can start at any of the five stages in the game and any level in a stage except five. If you choose Hard, you have complete control.

- *Level:* Set the Level within the rules (see Difficulty).

- *Stock:* Choose the number of jets. The more you have, the better. Whenever you enter a new level, you get new jets. When you crash, you lose a jet. When you lose all your jets in a level, you can kiss Plealos good-bye.

- *Fire:* Choose Rapid fire for a rollicking good game or go with Normal for a game that's tough enough for most players.

- *Music and Sound:* For your listening pleasure, choose from 21 tunes and 43 special effects.

- *Exit:* To leave the Configuration Mode screen, select Exit. Press the A, B, or C Button then the Start Button to begin your mission.

In this space journey, there are five levels (with some divided into stages). Here's the space map:

- *Level 1, Stage 1:* Outdoors in the country side high above the Planet Nebula

- *Level 1, Stage 2:* Inside an enemy port

- *Level 2, Stage 3:* Free again and flying among skyscrapers

- *Level 2, Stage 4:* In the underground highway that leads deep inside the Planet Nebula

- *Level 3, Stage 5:* Wandering in a cave that is open

- *Level 3, Stage 6:* The smelly abandoned pipe

- *Level 4, Stage 7:* Among the statues inside the planet

- *Level 4, Stage 8:* Venture among the ancient ruins
- *Level 5:* Plealos. What came earlier was easy!

The even-numbered levels are horizontal and the odds are vertical.

Now, here's some more information about using superweapons.

Twin-Shot shoots two rounds forward, you get the maximum firepower up front. Use it in lower, horizontal screens where nobody is chasing you.

Back Fire is great on vertical screens to kill uglies you may not notice.

Five Wave is a good killing weapon since all five streams of fire come out in a wave and wipe out everything in front of you.

Destroy fires in only three straight directions so you'll miss some critical spots.

Thunder Force II

Wide Shot is good if you need to fire three in the front and one in the rear. Using Wide Shot, try to move your finger and thumb in a circular motion. That's the way the plane will fly. This sprays bullets in all directions. Also, it makes navigation in tight places easier. It doesn't hurt your ability to avoid bullets, and it tends to confuse the bullets that follow you.

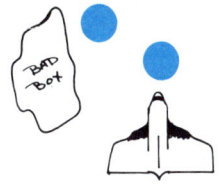

Hunter is great if you're a bad shot. It finds the enemy for you.

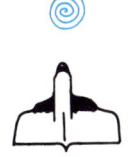

Clash sends out revolving missiles in the front.

Laser shoots two lasers in front.

Wave Shot blasts out missiles in a wave.

 *Side Blasters* fire ahead and up and down. This is necessary when you want to shoot the base in a horizontal screen.

 *Nova* is the way to go when you are being chased. It shoots missiles in three directions opposite from the direction you're flying.

 *Mega Flash* blasts out missiles in three directions in the front and to the back.

 *Claw* is more than a weapon. It creates a force field around your jet, and you're invincible while it lasts.

Breaker protects the Excelizer for a while.

Strategies

Hi's Hints

Thunder Force II is a tough game. Because it's such a challenge, I'm satisfied to stick to the lower stages. My best hint is that it doesn't pay to be in a hurry because you are not racing against the clock.

Getting and using weapons is the way to stay alive. You can get more than one weapon at a time. The ones you have show up on the top of the screen (along with the number of jets you have and the scores).

I change my strategy depending on whether the screen is horizontal or vertical. In vertical screens (Levels 1, 3, and 5), I get weapons by taking on the big superbases. I run in and shoot the middle and then kill the blue figures that appear. Finally, I fly right over the stars with the letters inside. The letters in the stars indicate which weapon you're getting. Once you have them, use the C Button (for Choose) and begin to use your new weapons.

In the horizontal screens (Levels 2 and 4), the weapons aren't under the superbases. Instead, they are inside that fat little starship. Fire off screen when you come on the screen, and you may get him before you get on the screen.

My technique is to run as much as kill. Shoot to kill. Drop back to avoid. I also hold the B Button down so the game shoots automatically.

Tec's Tips

This game is a challenge. You can play it a long time without getting bored.

To move, I press the controller and let it go. Even though the game is hard, the pattern is similar in the different levels. If you don't know where to go in a level, look for common patterns like four bases around a moving wall or six lines from one base to another. Think of patterns, and you'll find the fun.

As the levels advance, the familiar villains are there (sometimes with increasingly bad behavior) along with some new ones. You'll get attacked from the back even in horizontal levels.

When the mad dogs start nipping at you from all over, hover where there is the least danger. Move between danger on the top and bottom to give yourself a better chance of killing the villains.

There are dangers at each stage.

In Level 1/Stage 1 (sky), parts of the walls occasionally go away to let you go to the other side. I go back and forth because villains frequently come up from behind. Stay ready to dodge. The red dots are the very dangerous enemies. Running into skyscrapers and walls can kill, but I've been killed by red dots most often. A really nasty character is the circular figure that breaks into four pieces. Avoid this one at all costs.

In Level 1/Stage 2 (enemy port) avoid the red crab and ugly spaceship. Look out for its shots because it's brutal. In Level 2/Stage 3 (skyscrapers), you really get your wings. Now you can fly in eight directions instead of four. Just be careful not to run into skyscrapers. Check out the height of the skycrapers before you fly over them.

As you get started in Level 2/Stage 4 (highway), stay alive by following the highways with light blue lines. There are many opportunities to kill on the way, but you should go for the big bases, which will yield weapons. You can go through some walls in more than one direction, but beware of the weaving walls along the skyscrapers. They're murderous.

In many of the stages up to Stage 5, avoid the red seashell assassins that shoot red dots. As in other parts of the game, the small blue figures are friendly. Watch out for the robot with two arms and avoid the tank. As you drive through the maze, don't stay in the dark area too long, or you may be killed. That nasty neighbor from

Thunder Force II

Level 1 that divides into four pieces continues to reappear.

Things begin to get more complex as you rove through bases on the top—silos drop bad stuff and gates require perfect timing if you expect to pass through them. Glowing dots will seek you out, and you must shoot them. In earlier horizontal screens, it is okay to shoot only forward. But in these later horizontal screens (since there are guys out to get you from behind), shoot backwards as well.

Finally, Level 5 is a not so neighborly call on Plealos, the fortress. You'll learn to dread the fortress. It is so large that you can see only a small piece at a time. Shoot the turrets and run. Then run and shoot the turrets. Since you know the location of the fortress, you can keep firepower in front when you advance then shoot from the rear when you run away. You won't find what you need outside the fortress so look for areas you can fly into. But be careful because some are death traps. Others (especially those on the top) contain many turrets. If you shoot enough of these turrets, you get an opportunity to get the firepower.

More Power Pointers

- When it appears, dodge the red crab and the shots it sends.

- If you think it would be fun to find the edge of the world, consider these two problems. First, there is often a wall on the way that will kill you. Second, the world sometimes wraps around. You fly and end up coming back to where you were.

- In Level 5, follow the line of the bullets from the fortress to see the gun locations on Plealos.

Manufacturer Information

Company: Sega of America, Inc.

Address: P.O. Box 2167
South San Francisco, CA
94080

Game Counselor Hot Line: 415-871-GAME
(Please remember this is a regular toll charge telephone call.) 6 a.m. to 8:45 p.m. Pacific Time Monday through Friday and 8 a.m. to 5:45 p.m. Pacific Time Saturday and Sunday

Typical Price: $54.99

Tommy Lasorda Baseball

Description

If you love baseball, you'll love Tommy Lasorda Baseball. You can control your pitch and time your hits. If you can't go out to the ball game, this game is a super way to play your own favorite team against your most unfavorite rival. But don't get too arrogant because the computer is a tough player.

Let's Play

The following buttons give you overall control of the game. Use them to control your play at bat and your play at field.

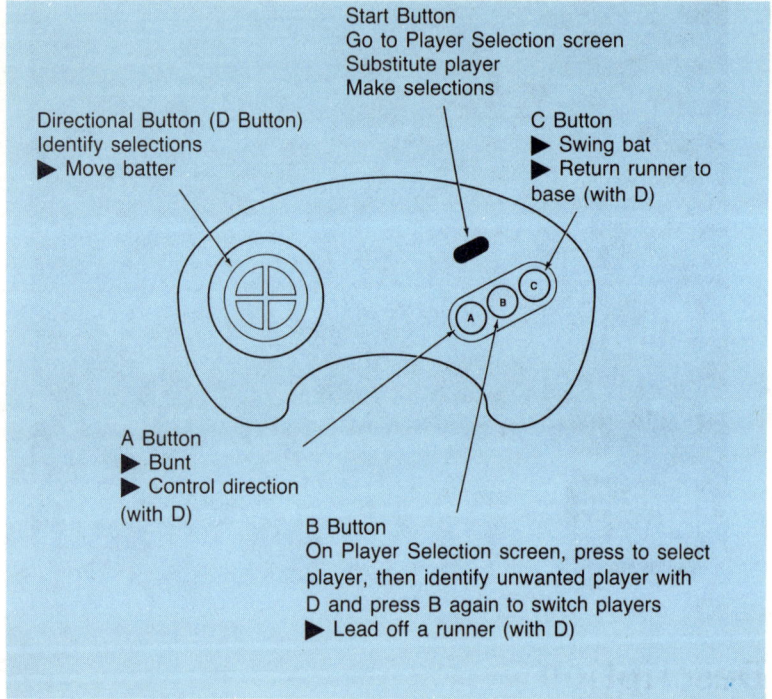

When you select your lineup from the Player Selection screen, the player data appears at the bottom of the screen. The scoop on pitchers includes:

- Name
- Earned Run Average (ERA)
- (R)ight or (L)eft handed
- Breaking ball break (A is greatest curve to D least curve)

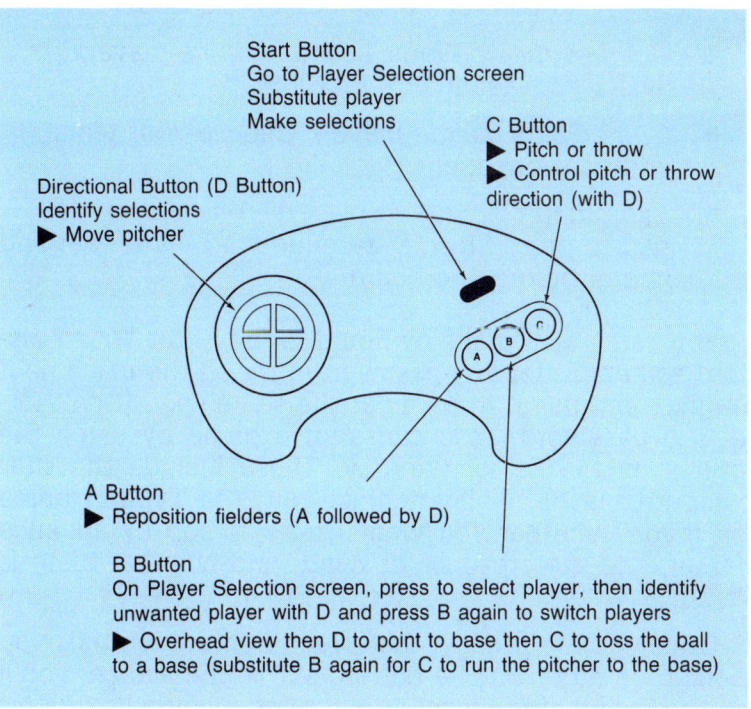

- Pitches before dead tired; number before signs of wear
- Throwing speed
- Distance hit ball will go (A is greatest and D is least)

The news on batters is:
- Name
- Batting average
- Number of home runs hit
- (R)ight or (L)eft handed
- Catching ability followed by throwing speed and running speed (A is best and D is worst in each case)

There are three types of games to choose from:

- *U.S. League or World League (single player):* Select your team and your lineup.

- *Open Game (single player):* Choose your team and your opponent.

- *Exhibition Game (two players):* Use Player 1's pad to press Start. Determine your own team and lineup before you begin.

You can stop a game by going to the Enter Your Password screen. Enter any password, turn off the machine if you like, and use it to begin at the same spot. (Don't forget the password.) You can alter a game by using the options on the Select window. These include the CPU (computer) level of play against you; the Type of game you favor; whether you want Errors, a pop fly advance Marker, and the presence of Wind; and whether there is Sound.

Once you are in play, the screen information tells you about the game. On the bottom left of the screen, you'll see the Speed of the most recent pitch followed by batter information. On the right of the screen, you'll see the inning, the score (batting team is marked with red), and the information on the pitcher.

Strategies

Hi's Hints

Regardless of which game you elect to play, one of the most important things to do is to pick the right team and the right lineup within a team. Batting average is not the most important factor. Foot speed for your runners on the base path is more important. Without good foot speed, you can't steal bases. You can steal bases on the pitcher only if you take off just as the pitcher begins the wind up, and then only if you've got a fast runner.

I think left-handed pitchers have an advantage in this game. So when you're picking your pitcher (whether it's a starting pitcher or a replacement pitcher), give the left hander a bit more consideration.

You are allowed to change pitchers and change batters, but it's the skill of your play that determines whether you strike the other people out and hit balls. Only in advanced levels of play does substituting pitchers or batters or bringing in a pinch runner make sense. I just go for having my best pitcher and my fastest runners in the lineup at all times.

These games tend to take a long time. Not only do the individual games get long, but also in some of the U.S. League and World League games, you go for maybe 30 games to determine the championship. I use the password feature to come back in the middle of a game in the series.

At first I got confused when the scoreboard showed only a single digit when there'd been double digits scored. Then I realized that the total is correct even though the individual inning shows only up to nine runs on the scoreboard.

I don't win much on this game, but I'm not so competitive that I get mad when I lose. Tec, on the other hand, gets moody when he loses. I look at it this way. A good inning is where they only score two or three runs. In a bad inning, they score in double digits. A good inning is where I get one or two runners on base. In a bad inning, I don't get anybody on base. What matters is that I had a good time.

Tec's Tips

I've worked and worked for overall strategies to improve my play on this. Hi swears that it's the lineup. I think the game is in the pitching and batting.

When you're at the plate to bat and the pitcher moves to either the left or the right, move the batter to the left or right as well. It will keep you squared up for the pitch. Never expect the game's pitcher to walk you. You have to swing the bat and hit the ball to get on base.

When you're batting, it's probably best to be farther back in the strike zone to give yourself the most amount of time. Also, set up on the same side of the strike zone as the pitcher on the mound. Then, look at a spot in front of the plate and not at the pitcher. You don't want to watch the delivery, you want to see the ball right in front of the plate as you're going to try to hit it.

There are two ways to hit the ball. One is to swing all the way through and the other is to tap the controller a little and partially swing and then swing away after that.

Bunting can be a good idea, but the fielders are so good that they'll throw you out. Also, when you bunt, you get more fly balls. The other side always catches fly balls. You can foul the ball. Of course, if you foul the ball on the third strike, you're out. The best time to bunt is when you have a runner on base. A sacrifice bunt will advance the runner.

When it comes to home runs, it's very difficult for us, the player, to hit a home run.

When pitching, you can't just throw straight strikes. If you give them a straight ball down the pike, they're going to hit a home run. Instead, you must curve the ball. It's best not to begin curving the ball at the start of the throw because you'll toss a ball. If you wait until your pitch is in front of the plate and then put some curve on it, you'll get more strikes, more ground balls, and more pop ups.

You should have your pitcher check the runners back to the base whenever they take a big lead. This doesn't happen very often. But, if you don't check them back, they will steal on you.

When you're on defense and there's a pop up, begin moving your players into position immediately. You can't wait until the ball comes back on the screen, or you'll never get there in time. After you play a while, you'll know whether it's short or long by the way the ball goes out in the infield. When you're fielding a ball, your fielder has to be exactly where the ball is going to land (or else you won't make the catch). Tommy doesn't give it to you on "close enough."

Also, the infielder should charge the ball (not wait for the ball but run in to meet the ball) and then throw it immediately to get those fast runners out. Immediately heave that ball in front of the runner. If you sling it behind the runner to a base where they've already been, you never catch them in a run down. Instead, they tend to score on you.

You can throw to the cutoff man to the outfield. That's usually quicker than trying to pitch it all the way home. From the infield, if you lob it right away, you can throw them out.

It's also a good rule to try to throw the runner out at first base. Because the other runners have a bigger lead off, it's pretty difficult to throw them out.

When I pitch, I mix it up. I move my pitcher's position on the mound just like the game does. And, I throw sliders or curves at the last minute to get strikes and to keep the other team from hitting so many long balls (especially home runs).

The advance skill leads the runner off the base. You can do this after every pitch. It's a lot of work, but it can give you a head start in terms of advancing the runners around the base.

The exhibition game is probably the most fun because in the regular game, the computer is very difficult to beat and I hate to lose. In the exhibition game, the two players battle it out against each other. Under those circumstances, the skill levels are likely to be more even.

More Power Pointers

- Look at the lineups for the teams in the other games. There's quite a bit of history, and some excellent players are involved.

- If you're having trouble getting hits or keeping up with your opponent, go to the Select screen and choose between the pitcher's, the normal, and the batter's game. The good thing about the batter's game is that you get some hits. The bad thing is that the computer gets even more hits. The pitcher's games tend to be lower scoring, but they can kill you at the plate.
- Wait until you're an advanced player to turn on the Errors and the hard Wind. It's hard enough to catch a pop fly with no wind or an easy wind. And the computer seems to always judge it right.

Manufacturer Information

Company: Sega of America, Inc.

Address: P.O. Box 2167
South San Francisco, CA
94080

Game Counselor Hot Line: 415-871-GAME
(Please remember this is a regular toll charge telephone call.) 6 a.m. to 8:45 p.m. Pacific Time Monday through Friday and 8 a.m. to 5:45 p.m. Pacific Time Saturday and Sunday

Typical Price: $59.99

World Championship Soccer

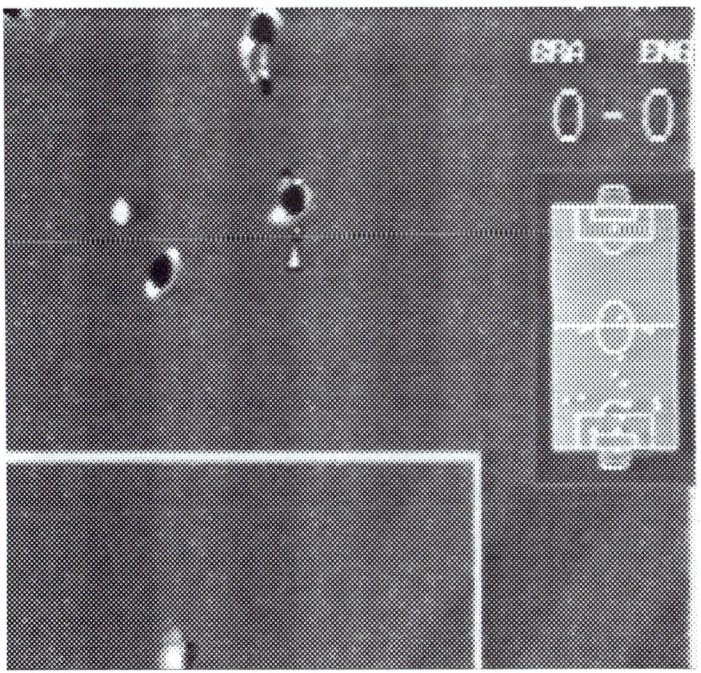

Description

Go for the World Cup against 24 teams. Practice, qualify, and play against the best. You weigh the offensive and defensive strategy when you select your team. With skill, timing, and Lady Luck, you're on your way to the Cup.

Let's Play

The following buttons give you overall control of the game. Use them to control the play.

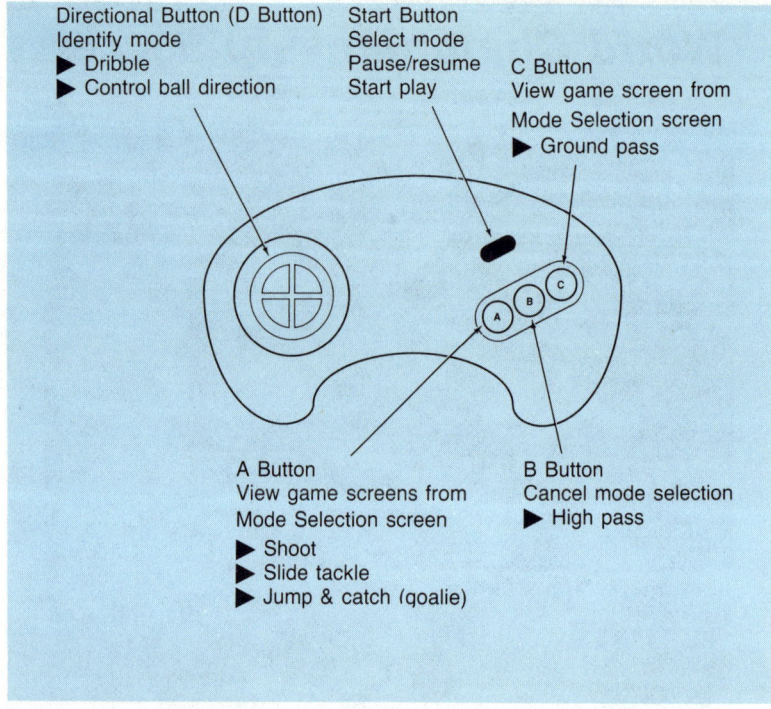

After the title screen, choose between three modes of play.

- World Cup
- Test Match 1P(layer)
- Test Match 2P(layer)

Throughout all screens, press the A or C Button to make a selection or the B Button to cancel a selection.

Next, the Team Selection screen shows up. Select a country and press the A or C Button to see the team data, which is ranked from 1 (lowest skill) to 5 (highest skill). Identify whether you want the team. Once you've picked your winning team, pick the 11 members of the team using the statistics presented. Go for the hot dogs.

If you are playing the World Cup game, the Elimination League screen shows up identifying what teams are playing. Once the league play is underway, you can return to this screen and select a team to see detailed information.

Watch the screen during play. You can check out the time elapsed, a blimp's view of the field, and the score. The team with the highest score in the allotted time is the victor.

Strategies

Hi's Hints

When it comes to picking your team, don't be a patriot. The teams are ranked from 1 to 5, where 5 is the strongest overall. The United States, China, and Japan are rated on the poor end as 1. To get an advantage, give the computer one of those teams and take a team rated in the top: Brazil, Argentina, Soviet Union, West Germany, or France.

For example, I play as Brazil and let the computer have China or Japan since they're tied for the worst. The consequence is that I have control over the degree of difficulty of the game and am making it very easy for me. Even in the round robin, if you pick the number 1 team in the world (Brazil), you have a tremendous advantage over the other team. When the teams are close, you don't have the advantage.

Choosing the members on the team is important also. They have rankings, and you need a strategy to figure out what player you want. Consider what you're good at and choose players that compliment your weakness. For example, after I played a few games, I found out that I'm not too bad at accuracy. I pick players that are better at other skills.

When picking individual players, the ones that are farthest forward (the offensive players) are the ones to whom you want to give the highest speed. Also, put a good kicker in for a forward player. Give the highest tackling ability to those players farthest back.

Overall, I like to look for players that are balanced. The players I choose don't have many 2s in their ranking. Instead, I pick the ones that have 3s, 4s, and 5s instead of an area of weakness.

Tec's Tips

When you're playing the game, you'll notice that the members of your team have arrows attached to them. This helps identify your players and the direction that you're going. There's also a big screen to the right that shows you what's happening in the match. This can help you to pick a direction to go down the field.

The game picks which of your players you are controlling with the D Button. You can make the game switch players by getting another player in front of the ball. Another way to get the computer to change it's mind is to run the current player off the screen. It will pick up a player that's in front for you to use as a defender.

On defense, I like to kick the ball downfield. To score, you often need to pass to a player outside but close to the goal and then to kick to the goal. Try getting goals both straightaway and in the corner of the net. In doing a corner kick, use the numbers 4, 5, and 6 because they go and curve and head toward the goal.

To steal a ball, use the A Button so you slide under a player and steal the ball away. It is hard to time, but if you keep tapping the button, you can do it. For beginners, it seems to be easier to move the ball down the field by kicking than by running. Use passing frequently when you get started.

Stealing the ball doesn't seem to work as well from the side. What you want to do is get in front of the player and then steal and kick right away. Getting the ball away consistently is the reason we want good tacklers in the backfield.

As you get more advanced, you'll want to run more with the ball, particularly if you notice on the big screen that there aren't many players in front of you. You want to kick down the field in general. But, when you get close, you don't want to do the long kick. Run and use the short kick. Otherwise, you'll find yourself kicking over the top of the goal post.

Avoid kicking when there's a defender in front of you. You need to wiggle to get around them to make an open path. Otherwise, they're going to steal the ball.

In general, keep the direction arrow down in the way you'd like the ball to proceed. If you're running with the ball, you have to make some fakes, but, typically, they are few.

More Power Pointers

- Ball placement on the field can be important. When on defense, keep the ball away from the middle of the field. You don't want them to get easy shots on goal. You want them to have to kick. On the offensive end, try to keep the ball in the middle of the field in front of the goal.

- When you get in trouble and don't know what is going on, press the Pause Button. It allows you to figure out what to do next.

- If you're the goalie, it can be hard to stop what's going on. Many shots are high, and you have to use the A Button to jump and catch.

Manufacturer Information

Company: Sega of America, Inc.

Address: P.O. Box 2167
South San Francisco, CA
94080

Game Counselor Hot Line: 415-871-GAME
(Please remember this is a regular toll charge telephone call.) 6 a.m. to 8:45 p.m. Pacific Time Monday through Friday and 8 a.m. to 5:45 p.m. Pacific Time Saturday and Sunday

Typical Price: $39.99

Zoom!

Description

Zoom! appeals to youngsters and oldsters. Though chasing, killing, and destruction is going on, it is so silly it will make you laugh.

The villains here are Phantoms who have surrounded our Mother Earth with a magic force field. You're the hero, Mr. Smart, who is out to zoom around Earth to save it. You will capture squares without running into the Phantoms or falling in the black hole. The ammunition is the phenomenal weapon all world superpowers should use: the rubber ball.

Let's Play

The following buttons give you overall control of the game. Use them to control Mr. Smart.

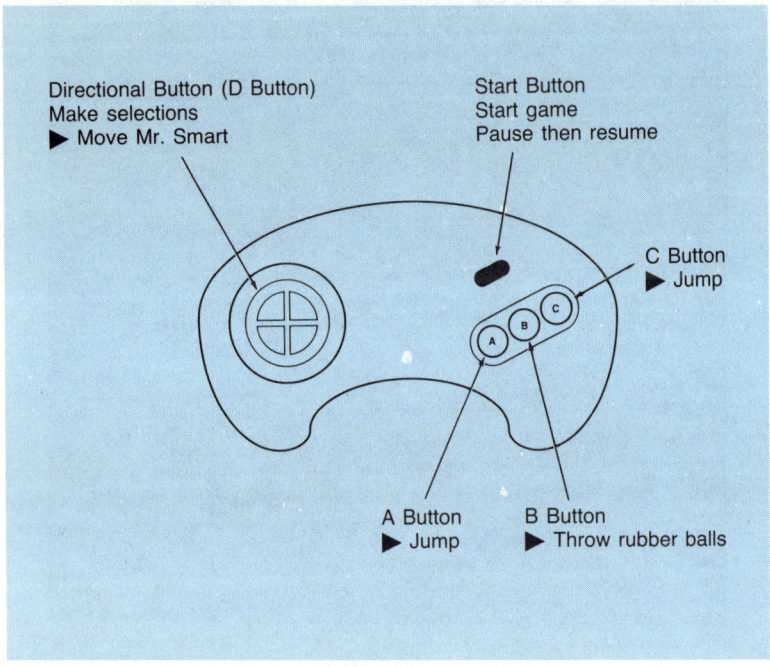

There are three play modes. When there are two players, Mr. Smart is yellow for player 1 and blue for player 2.

- 1 player
- 2 players with one or two control pads
- Competition for two players

The top of the screen shows the number of rubber balls left (the symbol shrinks and grows) followed by the number of lives. You get four lives to start and gain another life at 1,000, 3,000, and 5,000 points. Making adjacent squares flash also gives you lives. Phantoms take your lives from you.

Zoom!

At the top of the screen, you can also check the current stage and field under the score. The countdown timer is in the center top of the screen. When you get close to 000, do as much as you can since you have little time to lose!

Like most Sega games, press Start at the Continue Game screen to begin again at the first field of your last stage.

Zoom around trying to get the squares to flash. The points are awarded for flashing squares as follows:

- 10 points—Cross one line for a flashing square.
- 40 points—Cross one line for two flashing squares.
- 10 points times the number of squares—Make a line for single squares to flash.
- 40 points times the number of squares—Make a line for pairs of squares to flash.

Like any bad guy/good guy game, you have to know the players. These are the Phantoms that will be the curse of your existence:

 *Rowdy Fingers* is after you.

 Spiler (looks like a tomato sitting on a scrub brush) erases your hard fought for lines.

 Cue (looks like a molecule or a bunch of grapes) goes side ways to catch you.

 Spine-Spine (resembles a sea urchin) shows up anywhere.

 *Charm* (another sea urchin) is a charmer and will slow you down.

You're not alone in this wacky world. In addition to a star, which can be any treasure (or a way to get out of Stage 1), these are the goods to go for:

 Banana slows the Phantoms.

 Hourglass stops the Phantoms for a while.

 Sun makes you invincible for a while.

 Mushroom speeds you and gives you extra points.

The force field is won when all squares flash. There are six stages with six force fields in each. Your work is cut out for you.

Strategies

Hi's Hints

Zoom! is basically a game of evasion and accumulating the treasures. Unlike many of the other Sega games where you run over and kill the villains, you're trying to keep away from the villains and pick up some treasures to help you do that. Your mission is to surround all the squares by driving around them. It's not that different from eating all the dots on a screen in Pac-Man.

Getting the treasures is a very important part of the game because they make dealing with the Phantoms much easier. It's a big benefit if you can stop or slow Phantoms, speed them up, or have the screen to yourself.

The treasures are on the screen for only a short while, so you have to hurry. You can get new treasures while the effects of the old ones are still with you. If you use a combination of the treasures, you can clear much of the board without having to do much with the Phantoms.

Plan your moves carefully. Just because some treasure has the Phantoms moving slowly or frozen in place doesn't mean you can drive over the line that they're sitting on. You'll still die. The only exception to that rule occurs when you get the sun. It makes you indestructible so that you can drive on the line on which a Phantom is sitting.

My favorite treasure for powerful play is the star because you can get many extra squares. Instead of just driving around a square and crossing one line for only 10 points, I try to get all the sides covered except for one edge and then make a big long run in sequence for more points. One of the best moments in the whole game is to zoom down one long set of lines with a Phantom chasing you and finish the whole level.

Under all circumstances, whenever you see the wing, run over and get it. If you have to make two or three jumps or take some chances, do it because it wipes out all the Phantoms and the force field is yours.

Tec's Tips

Your ability to jump is one of the most important evasive techniques. Whenever you're trapped in a corner, it's usually easier to jump over a Phantom rather than to figure out which way it's going to go and then run away. You can also lead the Phantom away from where you really want to go by jumping. It will follow you and then you can make one or two jumps to get way over to the other side of the screen and do what you wanted to do. Another good time to jump is when you've covered all the lines in your area. Just jump over to the new section.

I tend to keep my finger on the Jump Button as opposed to the Rubber Balls Button. It's more useful in general to be able to jump than bonk (although bonking has it's moments as well).

To use the rubber balls well, get the Phantom directly behind you. Phantoms often try to cut you off or be around a corner so that the rubber balls won't do much good. When a Phantom starts to get close, take off in one direction and then bonk him with a rubber ball. It also helps to get Phantoms in a long line because they get bonked all the way to the other end of the line.

When you've played for a while, you'll find a good starting pattern for every screen so you'll be able to get as many of the squares flashing as possible. You'll also be familiar with the dangerous areas and should try not to go into those areas with a Phantom on your tail unless you have a specific strategy for dealing with it.

You cannot accidently jump off the field. The single exception is that you can jump for a treasure when it appears outside of the field. If you can get it, you sometimes get a special surprise.

It's not necessary to hold your finger on the Directional Button to go in the desired direction. If you're passing near a Phantom on the left or right, take your finger off the directional arrow for a moment and you're sure to drive right on by. But, do not wiggle your thumb accidently and head off toward the Phantom. You'll be cannon fodder if you do.

Some of the Phantoms are worse than others. But the Spiler (which looks like a tomato on a scrub brush) is the worst one of all because he erases the lines that you've already put down. This can really hurt your goals and objectives.

It's very important to practice using the Directional Button. Pressing on the diagonal can get you into trouble. It's a good way to go around a corner fast, but it's also a good way to accidently go around a corner that you don't want to go around.

As a general rule, it's better to cover the screen in long runs in the same direction, almost like a checkerboard. Then when you run across the screen in the other direction, you get long strings of squares completed at the same time. This gives you bonuses, and if you can get a large enough number on them (it seems to be a number in the area of 8), you get an extra life. Another reason to go for long strings instead of wiggling back and forth is that a wiggling approach tends to leave the sides of squares half drawn instead of completely drawn.

Unlike other games, where the Pause Button is useful only if you want to go and get a soda, Zoom! is very helpful in terms of strategy and showing you where you are and what's going on. Pause gives you a chance to see what is left undone on the screen, what's in your way, and what direction you want to take. Pause doesn't cost you anything and it may be possible for you to come up with a better strategy or find the last square or two that you haven't surrounded.

More Power Pointers

- Though time is involved, time is not the most important factor. Erase all the lines and get to the next level for the most points.

- The round doesn't end when the time elapses. What happens is that the Phantoms start to get you, and it's very tough to survive after that. You do get points for the remaining time that you have left. Take your time and stay out of trouble because when you run out of lives, the game is over.

- You start each field with new lives, and extra lives do not carry over into the next one. If you are close to being done on a screen and have lives, take some risks.

Manufacturer Information

Company: Sega of America, Inc.

Address: P.O. Box 2167
South San Francisco, CA
94080

Game Counselor Hot Line: 415-871-GAME
(Please remember this is a regular toll charge telephone call.) 6 a.m. to 8:45 p.m. Pacific Time Monday through Friday and 8 a.m. to 5:45 p.m. Pacific Time Saturday and Sunday

Typical Price: $42.99

Part

two

Master System Games

Alex Kidd in Miracle World

Description

Datetime: Many galaxies ago. Location: The planet Aries. Scene: Alex Kidd studiously developing his command of Shellcore, the strengthening skill. Leaving Mt. Eternal (a kind of University of Shellcore), Alex runs into a dying man with a fevered plea: "Take this map and medallion of Sun Stone. Please, please, I beg, help the peaceful city of Radactian. Paper wraps stone. Scissors cut paper. Stones break scissors."

This is a curious message indeed. Not one to dismiss lightly a dying man's request and being an all-around good person, Alex sets out to help. How? When? Where? Travel along, my friend.

Let's Play

The following buttons give you overall control of the game. Use them to control Alex Kidd.

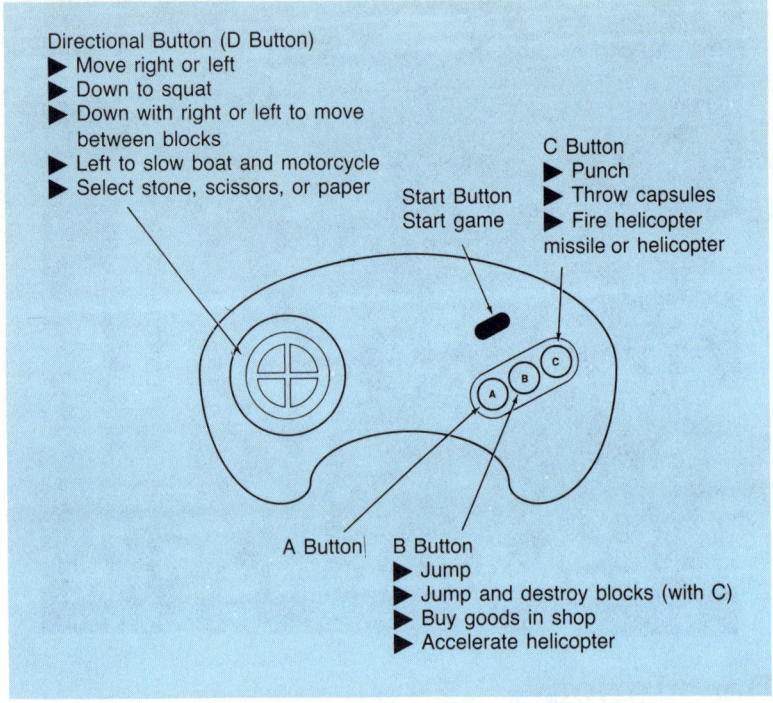

You'll soon learn that you have friends and enemies. Your friends include King Thunder, Saint Nurari, Patricia, Egle, High Stone, and Princess Lora. These are all pleasant-looking little people (with the exception of High Stone, but you'll know him by his crown).

Most of your enemies look like hands with feet. There's Parplin, Chokkinna, and Gooseka. Janken the Great (known as Janken the Rank by those who aren't on his social calendar) is the real villain and the Emperor of the planet Janbarik. He has a Nordic hat with a horn in the center and is dressed to invade Radactian. The other guys are his yes men. A number of different animals follow Janken.

You have to play Janken at his own game: scissors-paper-stone. You'll break blocks and, if you're lucky, find these treasures:

The Sun Stone Medallion

The Moonlight Stone Medallion

The Gold Crown (if you also have both medallions first)

The Hirotta Stone (related to unlocking the mystery of the crown)

A personal letter to the Kingdom of Nibana (you need to get some neat stuff)

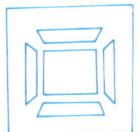

Boxes. You'll also run across boxes. If there is a star in the center, you get gold coins. If there is a question mark, you'll get a bracelet with which you can do waves of destruction, a new life, or a nasty ghost that you must escape. If you see a skull on a box, it's Pandora's—avoid it. If the box is pink and plain (no skull), check out the secret.

 *Telepathy Ball.* And, if that's not enough fun, go for the telepathy ball so you can tune in to what other people are thinking.

And if you still haven't had enough fun, shop till you drop or the game stops you. When you shop, check out these items (they cost gold coins and can't be used in water):

 *Teleport Powder* (100) to make you invisible

 *Power Bracelet* (100) for the Shocking Waves of Destruction (to be used in one location)

 *Alex Kidd* (500) for a new you

 *The Cane of Flight* (120) for your wings

 *Magic Capsule A* (100)—toss it for eight helpers—and *Magic Capsule B* (100)—pitch it for a safe boundary

Alex Kidd in Miracle World

Sukopako Motorcycle (200) to break rocks

Peticopter with weapons (200)

On your sojourn, you pass through 1) Mount Eternal, 2) Lake Fathom, 3) the island of St. Nurari, 4) the village of Namui, 5) Mt. Kave, 6) the Blakwoods, 7) Bingoo Lowland, 8) Radactian Castle, 9) the city of Radactian, 10) the kingdom of Nibana, and 11) Cragg Lake.

Use the subscreen to see your map, your assets, the number of your lives, and your score.

Strategies

Hi's Hints

This is a great game. I like to focus on the enemies. Each has its own way to be put out of the way. For example, on the second level, to kill Gooseka, first put stone then scissors. On the fifth level, Chokkinna can be wiped out with scissors then paper. Experiment with the combinations, then remember them. The blend of activity you take against an enemy will be repeated again in future play.

Every time you need to jump and punch, do it quickly. Otherwise, the enemies tend to get the upper hand, and you run the risk of losing a life. There are more points associated with hitting an enemy in a difficult spot. Of course, there is also more risk, so beware. I've played many times using the safer but less-points strategy as well as the risky go-for-the-points approach. I tend to get farther with a safer approach, but I had to take many risks to learn when the big points are really worth going for.

You'll need to identify how to move around certain obstacles. For example, in Level 3, if you hit the red balls with the propellers of the helicopter, you'll fall in the water.

When possible, always go for the money. You'll need it to shop at the store. Try out different purchases on different levels. I recommend buying a bike on the second level because it's much easier to get through the level with it. It seems unlikely, but try it.

Tec's Tips

I play for points. I get killed frequently, but that's the only way I've learned how to kill the enemies.

I always go for the boxes without skulls. There are very few that are too bad. Of course, you always want to run from the ghost in the question mark box. However, don't be misled, ghosts aren't always as bad as they seem. Like seeing the ground hog wandering around on Ground Hog day, it is good to see the ghost on the first level because you will be set up with an extra life. No ghost; no life.

There is one sure thing in this game. You can't get out of a level without getting the rice ball. Look for it and make sure you avoid the enemies who seem to guard it.

More Power Pointers

- You lose lives by losing the game to Janken or being beat to smithereens by the enemies.
- Get a life at the shop or find one in a box.

- When it comes to Parplin, Chokkinna, Gooseka, or Janken (the guys who like to play paper-scissors-stone), smack them on the head if you can (or dare). You get 2,000 points for the first three and 10,000 points for Janken.

- You get the following points for obliterating the enemy: 200 points for a monster bird, monster frog, scorpion, flying fish, small poisonous fish, rolling rock; 400 points for a bat, monkey, hopper, killer fish, sea horse; 600 points for a merman or ox; 800 points for a grizzly bear; 1,000 points for a rice ball; and 4,200 points for an octopus.

Manufacturer Information

Company: Sega of America, Inc.

Address: P.O. Box 2167
South San Francisco, CA
94080

Game Counselor Hot Line: 415-871-GAME
(Please remember this is a regular toll charge telephone call.) 6 a.m. to 8:45 p.m. Pacific Time Monday through Friday and 8 a.m. to 5:45 p.m. Pacific Time Saturday and Sunday

Typical Price: $39.99

Phantasy Star

Description

Phantasy Star is a space adventure in the Algol Star System. You'll need a passport to travel to each planet: earth-like Palma, dry Motavia, and icy Dezoris. You'll talk to villagers in their homes, replenish in hospitals, and resurrect your dead in churches. You can get money for hospitals and shops where you can buy strength (at hospitals and fast food shops), weapons, and tools.

Young Alis has vowed to revenge the death of her brother. Alis, armed with a sword, is in search of a gallant warrior named Odin. Alis travels with a party of friends to help. They may include Myau, a cat creature; Odin, also out to get King Lassic; and Noah, a wizard possessing many magical powers.

The enemies are Lassic and his Robotcops. They are formidable foes. Robotcops always need a special item for you to pass. They lurk, hunt, and only occasionally talk.

Let's Play

The following buttons give you overall control of the game. Use them to control Alis.

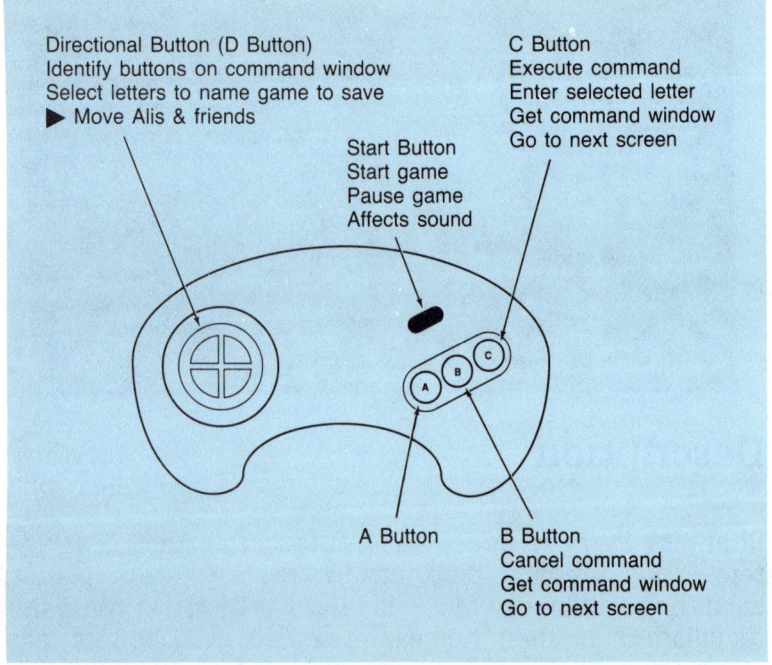

Since this game is complex (you can play it for many months), you will want to master how to save a game. You can save up to five games at a time. When you begin, you may choose to start a new game or continue a game that you've already named and saved.

To save a game, go to the Command window. Select Save and press the C Button. A list of saved games shows up in the upper right corner of the screen. Select a name to replace an existing saved game or select a blank on the list to go to the Name Registration option. When you register a name, use the D Button to select letters and press the C Button to enter the letter. To erase a letter, select Rub and press the C Button. Adv lets you advance one blank space. Select End when you're done.

To play a saved game, just choose Continue, follow the prompts, and select the name of the game you want to play. (If you say No at this selection point, you can delete a saved game.)

You'll use many menus in Phantasy Star. These are the codes for menus that appear when you are not in combat:

- *Stas (Status) menu* shows the power of each character with Alis. You can choose your characters and see the weapons and armor. You can also evaluate the character's overall level (LV—the higher, the better), the experience points (EP) for victories, the strength of attack (Attack), the ability for defending (Defense), the maximum hit points (Max HP) for surviving a battle, the maximum magic points (Max MP) for superior magic, and Mesetas (MST) or the amount of money the character possesses. By the way, you get experience points not only for victorious battles but also when you open a treasure chest. Treasure chests hold money and items—an arrow that hurts a member of your group or a blast that hurts you all. Be wary since two out of three spell T-R-O-U-B-L-E.

- *Magc (Magic) menu* shows the spells each character has learned.

- *Item menu* shows up to 24 gizmos that have been accumulated. When you use an item, pick the item then choose between these selections: Use (to use the item), Eqp (to outfit the character), or Drp (to get rid of an item you no longer want).

- *Srch menu* allows you to search the area in front of you. This way, you can uncover critical details.

The screen in combat will tell you the name of the monster (top), the characters in your party (bottom), and the battle commands that affect all members of the party (upper left). The battle commands are:

- *ATTK*—allows you to attack.
- *MAGC*—allows you to use magic assuming Alis, Myau, or Noah have learned spells. The spells appear for your selection.
- *ITEM*—allows you to select from the list of items to use in the clash.
- *TALK*—allows you to talk to a monster. Peace talks are always good to try out before flying off the handle with your fists.
- *RUN*—is the ever-present option to avoid a skirmish, if you can get away.

You can collect plenty of important items as you go. They are:

- *Transfer* to go to the last church you encountered.
- *Magic Hat and Sphere* to understand monster language.
- *Escaper* to become invisible.
- *Cola and Burgers* to up your HP.
- *Polymtrl* to melt materials.
- *Dungeon Key* and *Miracle Key* to unlock doors.
- *Hapsby Robot* to operate the Luveno.
- *Ambr Eye* in the forehead of the Casba Dragon.
- *Crystal* that contains magic to use against Lassic.
- *Roadpass* to let you board a moving road.

- *Passport* for interplanetary travel.
- *Compass* to journey through the forest.
- *Laconian Pot* that Myau needs.
- *Magic Lamp* to illuminate dungeons.
- *Flute* to get you out of the dungeons.
- *Gas SLD* to protect you from poison gas fields on Motavia.
- *Flashlight* to see your way through corridors.
- *Prims* to go where spaceships dare not travel.
- *Landrover* to speed around planets.
- *Hovercraft* to move across water.
- *Torch* from Dezoris to light your way.
- *Ice Digger* (needed on Dezoris) to go tunnel through ice mountains.

The spells are important to succeed in this game. A brief description of each follows:

- *HEAL:* Alis' way to fix illness and beef up HP.
- *CURE:* Myau's and Noah's approach to beef HP.
- *WALL:* Myau uses during battle.
- *PROT:* Noah uses during fighting to protect and avoid bad spells.
- *FIRE:* Alis and Noah use to scorch with fire.
- *WIND:* Noah practices to make tornado winds.
- *THUNDER:* A bolt of lightening from Noah.
- *ROPE:* Alis uses to tie up the bad guys.
- *BYE:* Alis uses to go away fast.
- *HELP:* Myau sends strength to others in the party.
- *TERR:* Myau makes weak enemies fearful.

- *TRAP:* Myau disarms traps in Treasure Chests and dungeons.
- *EXIT:* Myau uses to float to the top of dungeons, caves, and towers.
- *FLY:* Alis moves the group to the most recent church you encountered.
- *OPEN:* Noah uses to overcome the magic that seals some doors.
- *RISE:* Noah resurrects a lifeless party member.
- *CHAT:* Alis translates monster language.
- *TELE:* Noah uses to talk with a monster in his language.

Strategies

Hi's Hints

Save your game as you go, or you'll have to start all over when you are killed. If you save, when you restart, you get to start where you ended. Also, don't think about saving when you're up to your elbows in combat. You can't save during a scuffle so save when things are calmer.

Because the game has many places you can go, it helps to draw a map of everyplace you go. If you keep a map and write down hints you get as you go, you can use them later to improve your game. The Genesis Phantasy Star II game comes with a 120-plus page book and plenty of maps. The same approach is useful to this game (but not provided by Sega).

I usually shop at all the stores. That way I can get things I'll need later on. When starting, I also go everywhere to look for hints. It's a real discovery game. The game is similar to King's Quest on a computer. You have to do quite a bit of detective work before you defeat Lassic.

Don't get discouraged when you feel like you are stuck in a maze or dungeon. If you continue to explore them even after you fall in, you'll get to other areas.

 *Tec's Tips*

This is one great adventure with many routes through the game. You have to look for clues, magical items, weapons, and armor. Friends will help, and enemies will try to get you.

You must find your three buddies—Myau, Odin, and Noah. You can't do it alone and need their help to get through. Also, to get through, develop strategies to deal with each monster. A type of weapon or magic will work best for each.

Have fun through the game. After you kill Lassic, you will need to find the governor. You'll be in a maze or dungeon and will need to do your best to keep Maya alive. If that's a problem, you'll need to have a transfer in tow to Palma. Once you manage to get into the big mansion, you run a major-sized risk of tumbling into a pit. It's okay though because you can follow the halls and fall into two more traps. Go right and take two corners. Then, take a few steps and look at the left wall. Soon, a secret door will materialize before your eyes. Go right through the door and follow the hall to a magic door. Take a deep breath. It is through this door that you'll face your final adversary. Beef up first for strength—you'll need it!

There are many different weapons. Here are some notes on a few. The Iron Axe is powerful, but you need plenty of strength to use it. Odin (and only Odin) can use the Needle Gun and the Laconian Axe. Noah should use the Wand. Toss the Ceramic Sword to either Alis or Odin. Myau can use the Silver Fang.

You'll have many choices of armor. These are a few hints on a few of the types. Get Alis some armor right away. She can't go for long without it. For Odin, go for something really heavy, nothing lighter than Zirconian

Armor. Thick Fur is the only thing little Myau can use. The FRD Mantle is a gift from Master Tajima for Noah.

Shields are numerous and provide extra protection. Look for these. Leather isn't good for anyone. Go for the heavier materials, but remember that Alis can't handle heavy metals such as Bronze. Laconian is best for her; make sure she takes Laconian to the party with Lassic. Odin needs the Mirror Shield. And our fluffy friend Myau can use only gloves.

More Power Pointers

- Any time you have trouble, check your STAS to see how much damage your group has undergone.
- Don't go for leather anything, if possible. It isn't a good defensive material.

Manufacturer Information

Company: Sega of America, Inc.

Address: P.O. Box 2167
South San Francisco, CA
94080

Game Counselor Hot Line: 415-871-GAME
(Please remember this is a regular toll charge telephone call.) 6 a.m. to 8:45 p.m. Pacific Time Monday through Friday and 8 a.m. to 5:45 p.m. Pacific Time Saturday and Sunday

Typical Price: $69.99

R-Type

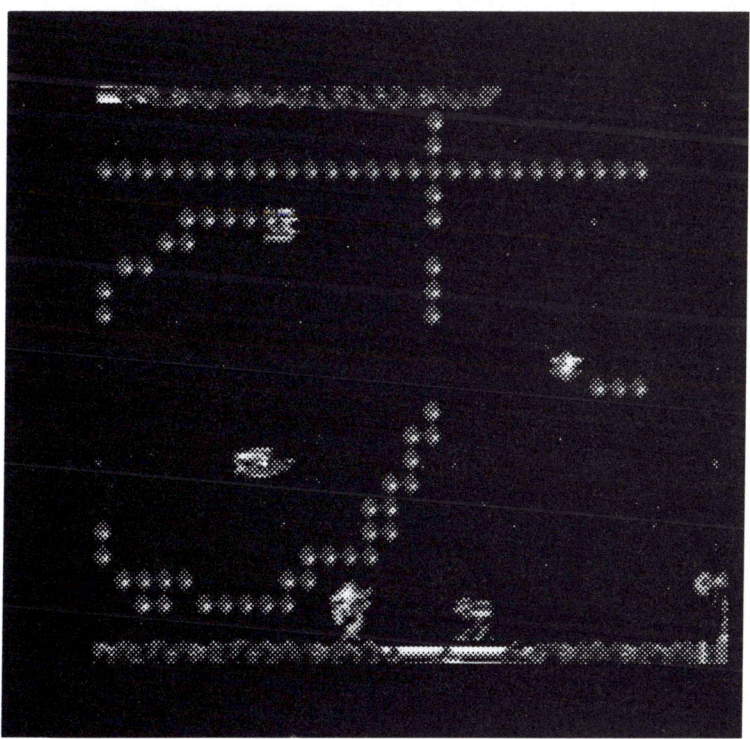

Description

Space may be your final frontier unless you can pilot the R-9 spacejet to triumph against the Bydo Empire. The stakes: the future of planet Earth. The Earth Defense League has summoned you to pilot the R-9, the state of the art in space warfare. The competition will come at you fast and furious. You must keep your wits and win the war.

Let's Play

The following buttons give you overall control of the game. Use them to control your spacecraft.

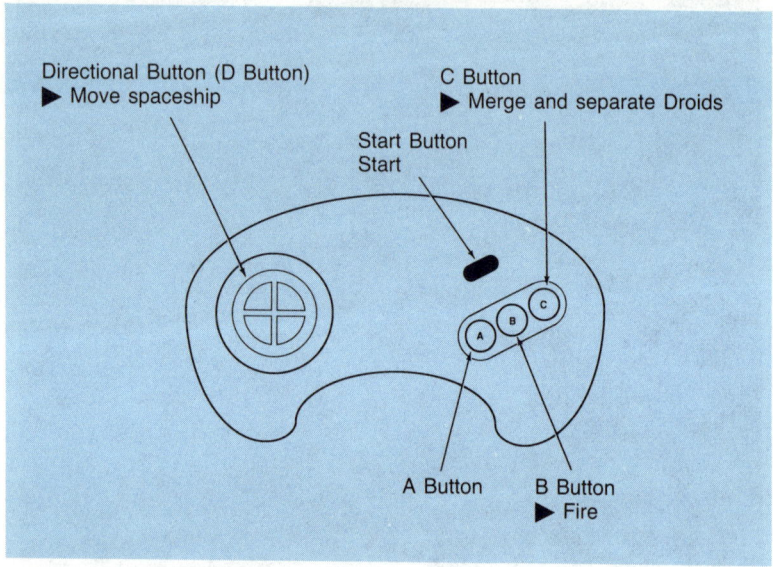

The R-9 is a sophisticated spaceship. You get three to use during the game, compliments of the Earth Defense League. Additional R-9s appear at 50,000, 150,000, 250,000, 400,000, and 600,000. The score and number of ships remaining appear at the end of each stage of the game.

There are eight stages to the play:

- *Stage 1:* Flirt with the Bydo Empire's first base
- *Stage 2:* Move within the Bydo caves
- *Stage 3:* Face the Mega Battleship
- *Stage 4:* Meander through the Terrible Mechanical cells
- *Stage 5:* Cruise the underwater caves
- *Stage 6:* Dart in the warehouse labyrinth

R-Type

- *Stage 7:* Sneak around the eroding city
- *Stage 8:* Confront the Bydo Empire Home Base

To protect and assist, use the sphere-shaped Droid units that you acquire when you fly through the blue force gem. Use the buttons to join a Droid to your R-9. Use the Droids to line up for battle. Shooting power with Droids is as follows:

- Laser power depends on the number of Droids you have and whether they are attached to your ship.
- When you have a second blue force gem, the Droid can shoot pulse beams up or down as long as it isn't attached to the R-9.
- Get a third blue force gem, and the Droid can fire pulse beams not only up or down but diagonally up or down.

To power up your R-9, shoot POW Armor units. These powers may be yours:

- The blue Reflecting Laser Force Units allow you to fire a laser beam that bounces off your target.
- The red Antiair Laser Force Units discharge rings straight ahead.
- The Speed Units (identifiable by the S) increase your speed.
- The yellow Antiland Laser Force Units shoot up and down and run alongside objects.
- The Twin Missile Units (identifiable by the M) fire twin missiles that find your target.
- One or two Bit Units (round spheres) may be attached to the R-9 to shoot and destroy on contact.

Strategies

Hi's Hints

In R-Type, you advance through stages and unearth new enemies to deal with. Your strategy is to identify the best way to kill your enemies. For example, old Vin is indestructible. You can shoot all day and not kill him. There are other enemies that you can kill but that are so difficult to kill, you end up losing your life and wondering why you took them on.

At the end of most stages, you'll find a ferocious boss that you'll need to kill. For example, at the end of Stage 1 is Krell who has a little face in the middle of a body that's mostly tail. Just shoot his face to get on with the game. That sounds easy enough, except his tail is always in the way.

Gomanda greets you at the end of Stage 2. He's got an eye that is mostly shut, but when the eye opens, blast it and you'll move on.

Mega Battleship (guarding the end of Stage 3) will send plenty of blasts your way. If you get under the ship and shoot at what looks like a little plunger and is officially called the "upper piston," you can destroy the battleship.

In Stage 4, you'll run into Monpaira (where do they get these names?). Junk comes at you from this conglomeration of spaceships. When the pieces come apart from the whole is your opportunity to attack. Kraken (Stage 5) has a red spot in the center; this is its weaknesses. Buronku in Stage 7 is actually easy to get. Don't let the snow drop on you and go for the blue spot on this creature.

In the last stage (Stage 8), you've got a real brawl in front of you. The hot shot, Mr. Bydo himself, is there to stop you from winning the battle at all costs. Go in armed with lives, firepower, and Droids. Surround Mr. Bydo and attack.

R-Type

The game will let you continue three times before it returns you to the beginning of the game. This makes it challenging to get very far. Although once you figure out the secret pattern, it isn't as hard as you might imagine to get through.

Tec concentrates on Droids. I concentrate on survival (with Droids) and on the pattern where the POW armor is located. The armor contains your power, which you need for extra firepower and speed and the ability to handle the Droids. Without the POW armor, you can't get anywhere.

I've also noticed that once you get the pattern in a level, the bad and good guys come pretty much at the same spot on the screen.

There is no real hard-and-fast rule about being on the left or right side of the screen. You'll be successful if you stay where the game starts you, which is left of the center of the screen. In this way, you can shoot and kill a long way in front of you and see what's coming. Don't go all the way to the left side since the enemies come on, shoot, and leave from that side. You tend to get killed before you even see what is happening.

Try to remain centered between the top and bottom of the screen. However, also try moving along the edge where the enemies tend to come out. You can kill them quickly. I play more or less on the edge and a little to the left as much as in the center.

It also pays to move up and down as you shoot. This will send out a spray of bullets instead of bullets in a line. You can kill more with this technique.

Tec's Tips

There are only two buttons that do most of the work in this game—the D Button (directional) and the B Button (firepower). I've found two ways to use the Fire Button. One way is to just push it to fire and kill. The other way is to hold it down for a while so it gets a super charge. This lets you kill more than one enemy at a time or use one shot when you otherwise would need two. The book that comes with R-Type says it's important to run your finger in a circular manner to find the secret superpower you might have. In fact, if you hit both the B Button and the D Button at the same time, this will work.

The C Button lets you determine whether your Droid is on the front or the back of your ship. It is also important to use with the B Button for the secret firing power. But be careful when you have Droids since the C Button is responsible for releasing and bringing in the Droids. You can be going for firepower and lose a Droid by accident.

In addition to determining your relationship with the Droids, the C Button allows you to fire a Droid at the sensitive part of the boss alien that lies at the end of the round. This will help you kill the foreigner.

The way to beat the bosses at the end of each stage is to combine your use of superpower and your ability to shoot, pull back, and shoot again.

The key strategy for this game is to acquire Droids by shooting shells. The Droids are you're best friends, and you're going to need all the friends you can get in this place. The Droids are important for more than one reason. Not only do they give you extra shooting power, but they can also protect you. For example, if you are hit on the end without Droid protection, you'll die. If you have a Droid, you'll be protected. I believe that there isn't a single Droid that isn't worth going after.

Overall, if you have limited Droid assistance, it's better to have your Droid in front of you than behind you because you're moving forward in the game. Most of your trouble will be coming at you. The Droid can protect you more in front. If you get it behind you, disconnect, drive around, and use that button to shoot it back in the front again. The real secret is to keep Droids both behind you and in front of you and shoot them out.

If I get pounded in the game, instead of restarting where I was, I go back to the beginning and start over to pick up more Droids for more power when I get to the more difficult parts.

When you go after the enemies in this game, don't always go straight at them. You can shoot them on the edge and kill them. You can kill by side-swiping, but you have to be careful. It's important to avoid being side-swiped yourself. I tend to use side-swiping as an offense and am careful in defense. This also applies to the edge of the game. You can't just run into the walls anywhere you want. In some places it's safe, but in most places you'll die.

You must keep moving. Most of the shots by the enemies are directed at your position. Only your worst enemies will shoot rockets that follow you. So, if you keep moving, most shots will miss you.

You need to learn how to drive straight. It's easy to start wiggling all over, but you run into things. As you get more advanced (for instance in Stage 3), you have to drive straight through some small holes. To get through, you have to be very good at hitting the arrows to go exactly where you want.

Be conservative and don't get greedy. Those little 100 and 300 pointers won't help your fun in the game. Don't fly into matter or have close calls at the edge of the screen or approach danger for no good reason. Most of the fun and satisfaction in this game comes from getting a long way into the game. You don't have to clean up the entire screen to do that. You want to kill as many things as you can (some chase you if you don't kill them), but you can avoid quite a few things and live longer.

More Power Pointers

- At the beginning is a demonstration screen where you can improve your strategy by noting where your enemies come and go. It is good to see what's going on in the game.

- When you die, all your Droids and superpowers go away. Be evasive and patient because, once hit, you make a big sacrifice for continuing.
- A strategy for dealing with a number of creatures at one time is to fire while you're moving backward. You can shoot and move at the same time.

Manufacturer Information

Company: Sega of America, Inc.

Address: P.O. Box 2167
South San Francisco, CA
94080

Game Counselor Hot Line: 415-871-GAME
(Please remember this is a regular toll charge telephone call.) 6 a.m. to 8:45 p.m. Pacific Time Monday through Friday and 8 a.m. to 5:45 p.m. Pacific Time Saturday and Sunday

Typical Price: $49.99

Reggie Jackson Baseball

Description

Reggie! Reggie! Reggie! Go to the World Series with Reggie Jackson Baseball. As manager of one of the 26 major league teams, you select and maneuver players, pitches, and hits. You'll need all the skill you can get because you're up against the best; there are no farm teams here.

Let's Play

The following buttons give you overall control of the game. Use them to control play.

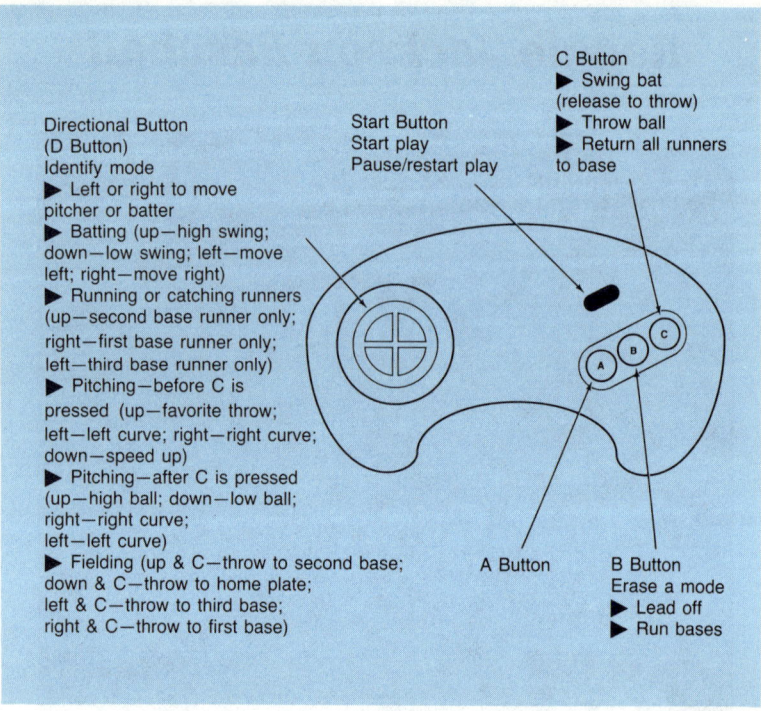

In this game, you can choose from four modes of play:

- *Exhibition Game:* This game may be played with one or two players. If you play alone, the computer picks a team to play against you. The Open Game means you can play the best two out of three.

- *Tournament:* To play alone, you pick a team and the computer matches up. Go on to the Division Championship, League Championship, and World Series.

- *Watch Mode:* Choose two teams and watch the computer battle it out. If you feel the urge to participate, you can jump in.

- *Home Run Contest:* There are 20 turns at bat for you or you and a friend.

Before the "Play ball!" shout goes out, you need to make some critical selections. Select between Auto Mode (the computer sends the fielder to the ball) or Manual Mode (you move fielders). Then, pick your team followed by your pitcher.

In the heat of play, a good manager uses all the information available. In the upper left corner of the screen, the balls, strikes, and outs are displayed in that order. In the upper right corner of the screen, the inning and score are shown. In the center on the left and right, respectively, the third- and first-base runners are shown. In the lower left corner, you can check out the data on your pitcher. In the lower right corner, the scoop on the batter is shown.

Strategies

Hi's Hints

I like this game better than Tommy Lasorda Baseball because it's easier to win. The graphics aren't as good, but it's easier to master.

There is a feature where the computer plays itself. When I first got started, I used this feature and watched what was going on for a while. The computer does try to throw the runners out on base, the pitcher does move around in the mound, and so on. From this, I learned alternatives to play, which I later used in my own play.

The game moves quickly. The Pause Button is useful to see what's going on and to figure out strategy.

Tec's Tips

In this game, it makes sense to pick the pitcher with the lowest earned run average. This means that they give up fewer runs.

You can't throw simple pitches for strikes straight across the base. You have to try to throw some different pitches. The strike zone is not all that easy to hit. The breaking pitches need to be used judiciously. If you always throw the same types of pitches, you're going to be blasted out of the ball park.

The best way to get a strike with your pitcher is to use the up direction on the D Button. This is the pitcher's favorite throw. Fast balls, curve balls, and speed-up balls seem to get hit more often and harder than the pitcher's favorite throw. So, make that throw the main course. Then make the dessert a curve or other pitch. You do have to change a little bit so the computer doesn't anticipate what's going on. But if you change it too much, it will be easier to miss the strike zone.

You can either bunt by swinging halfway or hit through the ball. You can also choose to swing high or low using the D Button. In general, it's a good idea to move left or right to be in much the same location in the batter box that the pitcher is on the mound.

You cannot pick a spot in front of the plate. You have to watch the whole pitch to see whether it's breaking and to figure out whether it's high or low. I find that many pitches are thrown in the middle of the strike zone and fewer are thrown high or low. Going with the average height will get some hits for you. But, when you see a pitch that is going high, stay high or you'll get a strike or pop up.

If you get three balls and have only one strike or no strikes, take a pitch just like in a regular game. This game will occasionally walk you. The computer will also hit you with a pitch that can be funny since it doesn't hurt. They come in with the stretcher to take you out, and everyone gathers around the pitcher. Actually, the practice of standing in the middle of the batter's box can be a wacky strategy.

The only reasonable way to learn how to hit high or low is to play the Home Run Contest game. The computer will beat you, but you will learn how to hit the ball better.

Hi and I watched the computer play itself, played the Home Run Contest, and then played the game. With that kind of practice, we were in a good position to play a contest.

The game does let you push the button to advance around the bases and run faster, I tend to be conservative about getting extra bases. The computer throws you out often when you try to turn that solid single into a squeaker double.

Be cautious at first about leading your runners off because the machine will pick you off. After a while, it becomes second nature to get that runner back on the base.

When fielding, a ball may be coming at your player but over his head so that you can't move him back in time. In this situation, there's no harm in pressing the D Button so he'll jump up for the catch.

Also when fielding, throw fast. If your baseman isn't in position, throw right past him. As you get started, use the Automatic Fielding mode rather than control the fielding yourself.

Any time someone hits a ball deep to the outfield, fling it back to the infield immediately. Don't worry about whether the infielder is in position. It takes so long to throw a ball from the outfield to the infield that your infielder will be there. It's only if a ball is hit shallow that you must be sure that you have someone to cover the base.

More Power Pointers

- Bunt by releasing the button as the bat goes over the plate.
- Don't miss the Home Run Contest. You get 20 turns at bat.

- When runners are on base, they automatically start to run when the ball is hit. Select them to make them run to steal or to return them if you sense an out is coming in the outfield.
- When you try to figure out what base to throw to, keep your eye on the little diamond that's superimposed on the screen in the lower left corner. It shows you where the runners are.
- Press the B Button, and a runner will lead off. After the pitch, press it again to steal.
- Keep pressing the B Button, and the runners will run faster.
- Use the C Button to return runners to bases. (Use the D Button to select a particular runner first.)

Manufacturer Information

Company: Sega of America, Inc.

Address: P.O. Box 2167
South San Francisco, CA
94080

Game Counselor Hot Line: 415-871-GAME
(Please remember this is a regular toll charge telephone call.) 6 a.m. to 8:45 p.m. Pacific Time Monday through Friday and 8 a.m. to 5:45 p.m. Pacific Time Saturday and Sunday

Typical Price: $49.99

Shinobi

Description

A master of Ninja Magic, you are a weapon in motion. You must battle with the Ring of Five to save the lives of children of the leaders of the world. In each of your five missions, you must defeat one of the leaders of the clan. Though you stand alone, they do not. Each level is guarded with hooligans and thugs. It's not a fair match. But it's your match.

Master System Games

Let's Play

The following buttons give you overall control of the game. Use them to control your action during the game.

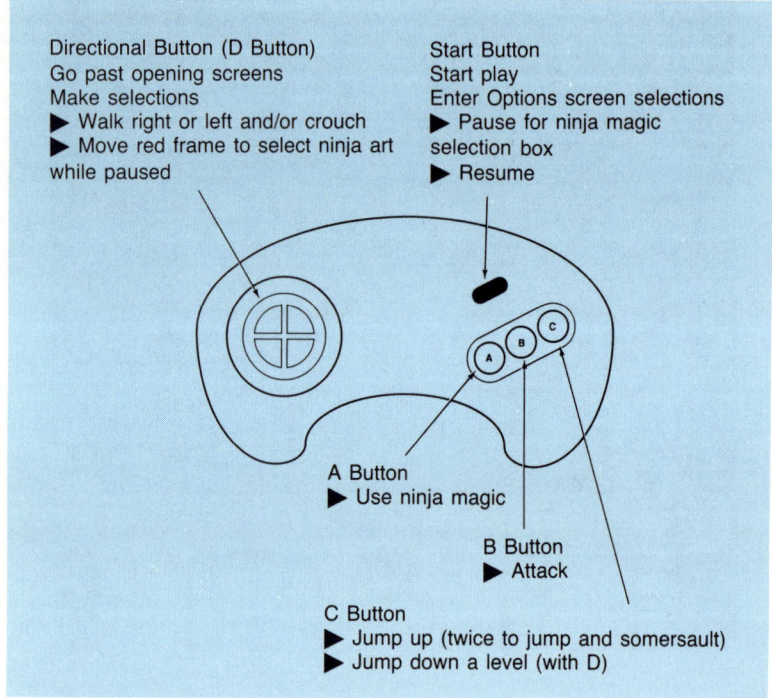

Directional Button (D Button)
Go past opening screens
Make selections
▶ Walk right or left and/or crouch
▶ Move red frame to select ninja art while paused

Start Button
Start play
Enter Options screen selections
▶ Pause for ninja magic selection box
▶ Resume

A Button
▶ Use ninja magic

B Button
▶ Attack

C Button
▶ Jump up (twice to jump and somersault)
▶ Jump down a level (with D)

As you progress in your purpose, news about the Ring of Five leader, his picture, name, whereabouts, and related code appear. The missions are:

- *Mission 1:* Ken Oh
- *Mission 2:* Black Turtle
- *Mission 3:* Mandara
- *Mission 4:* Lobster
- *Mission 5:* Masked Ninja

Each mission begins with your display of skill with the Shurikin (star weapon), which you use to keep the

138

ninjas away. You get Ninja Magic by succeeding in the round and 500 points for every ninja you render lifeless.

If you make it through the first round of the mission, the Ninja Magic (up to four types at a time) is shown at the top of the screen along with your score, life meter to show how much life you have left, and the number of lives you have left. When the left tile flashes (after killing ten bad guys), you can use the magic.

The six types of magic are:

- *Metal Binding Magic* to freeze the bosses
- *Invincible Magic* to make you unbeatable while you flash
- *Eight Hands Magic* to clone you eight times for fighting
- *Flying Squirrel Magic* to fly through the air
- *Lightning Magic* to use devastating lightning
- *Tornado Magic* for a whirlwind to protect and kill

You begin with three lives. At increments of 100,000 points, you get a new life. Go for all the life you can get. You'll need it, especially in later missions.

Hostage children appear throughout the game. These are the children of the leaders of the world who are innocent of any crimes and have been kidnapped for political reasons. Save the children. When you complete a recovery, you receive more power. These include:

- *Shurikin Power Up* for more damaging Shurikin action
- *Restore Life Meter* to refill your meter
- *Life Meter Max* to top off your meter
- *Punch and Kicks Power Up* to make you a stronger foe
- *Bonus* to enter the Bonus (Shurikin-throwing) Round
- *10,000 points*

Strategies

Hi's Hints

This game is full of villains and bad situations. To win, you'll need all the extra weapons and power boosts you can get. Make sure to save every hostage along the way to get the help you need. Also, try not to miss the Blue Ninja because you get twice as much magic if you kill it.

Mongo (the guy with the tank top and shield) is a particularly evil opponent; you'll see him often. I've had good luck wiping him out like this. Hit him with the Shurikin. When he throws his big sword at you, hit him with another Shurikin. He's good for the maximum on the roughneck scale: 300 points. I go after him frequently with this technique and am usually successful.

Get the sword in the caves to use later to kill the frogmen with swords and tanks. They're only 100 points each, but you can use all the points you can get, and the sword is pretty easy to pick up.

The real battle is with the leaders of each mission. You have to get past them to move on. I've been keeping a very detailed diary on my encounters with these leaders.

The first very ungentlemanly gentleman is Ken Oh, the main man in Mission 1. To get him, try nailing him five times in the head. But be careful! He throws a mean fireball. In Mission 2, get the Black Turtle by shooting the nose of the helicopter a few times. That will usually take care of him. When you get to Mission 3, you're introduced to Mandara with all the hands. Run up, jump, and fire quickly. Shoot the fire-breathing head a few times in the eye, which is his weak spot.

Mission 4 is a killer. If you don't kill all the Flying Ninjas, you will die. You've got to be good, and it will take a few tries to get the pattern down. This mission has a Lobster boss. To get the Lobster boss, remember that he is weakest when he lowers his sword. I go for the face.

In Mission 5, you'll find out that the Masked Ninja is tough to get. He has different forms. When he glows, shoot him four times. When he is a tornado, kneel down and let him chase you. When he gets close, kick him three times. Then he'll jump at you. He does not give up! When he jumps and lands, a white shadow is behind him. Watch the shadow because it is as dangerous as the real thing. Jump every time he jumps and shoot him in the air. When you do this, the shadow will disappear. Shoot him in the air three times.

Finally, as if you aren't tired already, he comes in the Masked Ninja form. And is he mad! You must have plenty of energy to get through this one. Let him run past you once then shoot him fast and furious from afar. Keep shooting until you win.

Killing these leaders to rescue the children is what this game is all about. Points are good, and weapons are good. You need it all to complete your mission.

 *Tec's Tips*

Hi is the real expert on this game. In fact, I can't do better than her so I don't try. I do know a few pointers though. Always go for rescuing the kids. You can get weapons, points, or life maxes.

When it comes to weapons, some are good to use close up (Shurikin, long sword, nunchaku, and manrikugari chain). The knife, bomb, and pistol can be used from a distance. I prefer long-range weapons over the short-range ones.

I watch for patterns in attack when I play this game. You can anticipate where your enemies will go and blitz them in a good position.

More Power Pointers

- To start at any level, push down the controller at the main screen then press the A Button.
- The knife travels faster than a Shurikin.
- To make the bomb a time bomb, squat then shove it off.

Manufacturer Information

Company: Sega of America, Inc.

Address: P.O. Box 2167
South San Francisco, CA
94080

Game Counselor Hot Line: 415-871-GAME
(Please remember this is a regular toll charge telephone call.) 6 a.m. to 8:45 p.m. Pacific Time Monday through Friday and 8 a.m. to 5:45 p.m. Pacific Time Saturday and Sunday

Typical List Price: $44.99

Wonder Boy in Monster Land

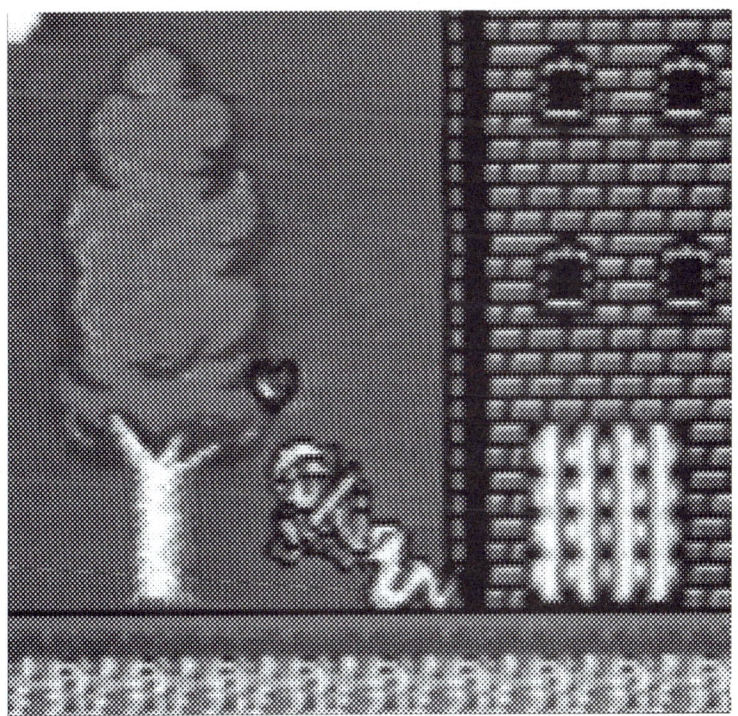

Description

This is no Alice in Wonderland. Wonder Boy's quiet little Wonder Land has been transformed into Monster Land by a dragon with a flame thrower for a mouth. As luck would have it, only Wonder Boy can return Monster Land to its Wonder Land state by knocking off the demons and monsters, especially the MEKA dragon.

Let's Play

The following buttons give you overall control of the game. Use them to control Wonder Boy as he goes about his duty.

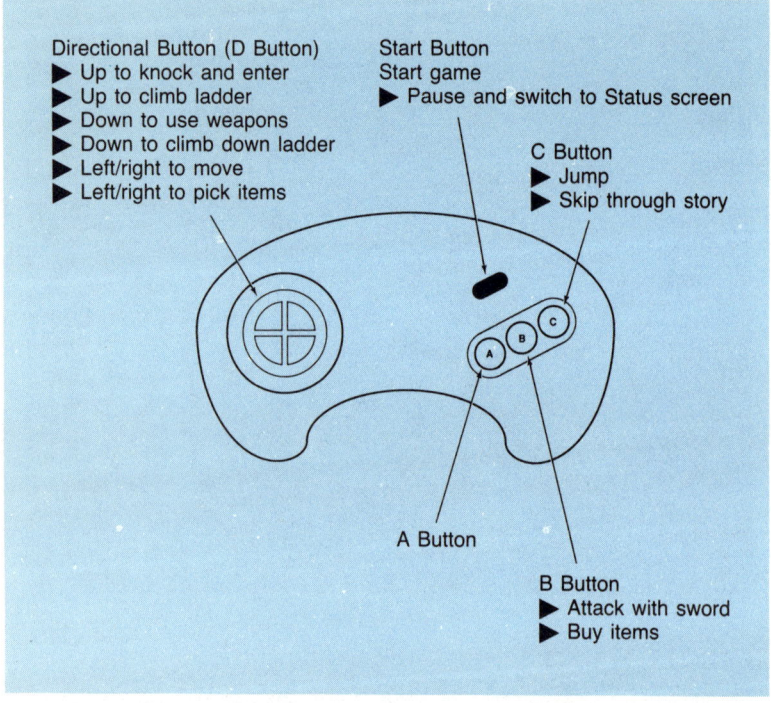

The 12 domiciles in the game follow: 1) City of Wonder Land, 2) Valley of Peace, 3) Wizard's Castle, 4) City of Baraboro, 5) Mam Desert, 6) Pyramid of Sphinx, 7) Pororo Islands, 8) Village of Cacti, 9) Floating City of Tonnovia, 10) Ice Castle, 11) Undersea Kingdom of Catfish, and 12) Labyrinth of No End. You have to get the key at each level to go to the next round.

En route to your destiny, you will come upon treasures. You'll find gold coins when you bash a monster or find it along your path. The gold water jug is worth 500 points, and the gold necklace is worth 1,000. Both can be gotten from destroying monsters. You can also locate all these other golden treasures stashed in hiding: scale (1,000 points), mirror (2,000 points), harp (5,000 points), and crown (10,000). An hourglass will start your timer over. If the sand runs out, you lose part of a life heart.

As you go on the adventure, you can get 16 possessions. An inventory is shown on the Status screen.

The Status screen identifies your possessions in several categories. This may include:

- *Safety equipment* such as the sword, shield, armor, and boots

- *Magic weapons* such as bombs to bowl at an enemy, tornados to envelope an enemy, fireballs to toss, and thunder flashes to get the bosses above

- *Special equipment* such as a helmet (for keeping your head in one piece: cost 25 coins), gauntlet glove (for super striking: cost 20 coins), and wing boots (for flying: cost 30 coins)

- *Unique items* such as revival potion to refill your energy at a cost of 100 coins, a robe-like mantle to make you invisible, a key to go to the next level, a flute, a star, a hero's emblem, a bell, a ruby to follow, and letters to ladies

The best treasure to find is a heart because it increases your life in proportion to its size. If you finish a round with all red hearts, you get 10,000 extra points.

Strategies

Hi's Hints

Nailing monsters and picking up treasures adds to your points shown across the top of the screen. At 100,000 and at every additional 100,000 thereafter, you get a new life heart. These are also displayed on the top of the screen along with the amount of gold cash available for buying the goods you need, the timer, and the types of weapons you have. I don't find time to be a big issue. Mostly, it's a game of finding what you need and learning the pattern.

Going on a shopping spree is easy early in the game. Naturally, you need money, which I typically find in clouds and trees. Once you have some coins, you can go into boot shops, armor shops, shield shops, and magic shops. It's not Saturday at the mall, but you can pick up some interesting stuff. The tougher the material for the boots, armor, and shields, the more expensive and better it is. The boot fabric is obvious. The other purchases range from poor to top quality often including these grades: light, heavy, knight, hard, legend. In boots and armor, you get what you pay for. If you have the money, go for quality. In shields, quality doesn't matter much. They all do the same thing: block the enemy that is shooting at you.

Have a blast shopping early in the game because it gets harder as the monsters guard the hard-to-find shops later. Some shops are impossible to find unless you fiddle around.

Actually, fiddling is the way to discover much about this game. I was exploring in the cave on the second level and found an interesting gem. While jumping above the lava, the screen says "there is something behind the wall." I just pressed up and found myself inside a door. Someone there gave me a scroll that could be used later on a higher level.

Tec's Tips

Killing monsters is my speciality. You have to play around to develop a technique that works with each monster. For example, the Death Master is worth 2,000 points and looks like a skull in a sheet with a scythe. When I see him, I stand still and wait for him to come down. Then I smack him with my sword. Once this happens, a key falls down. I get it and use it to get into the next level. I use this basic approach with every one of the many bosses.

A special technique seems to work on the knights (you'll know them by their swords). Get under them so they can jump on you. I know it sounds dangerous, but you have to be quick. Before the knight touches you, swing your sword to get him.

You'll get either a coin, heart, or weapon if you hit Snake, Python, Anaconda, Malkonid, Goblet, Goblin, Fang Bat, Vampire Bat, Eel Whips, Ghost, Jellyfish, Snapper Crab, Allee Rat, Master Rat, Madman, Tarman, Rohpah, or Octopus. You can use the coin for buying items in the stores. The heart can be little (for one heart back) or large (for all your hearts back), which, of course, extends your life. When you kill a monster, it is worth from 200 to 800 points according to type.

I recently developed a strategy for Level 12, which is the last, deadly level. You might not be there yet, but here's the way to do it once you hit that level.

First, find the dragon, go to the right, and go down the first well. You'll come to a split in the well. Go to the right. When you land on the ground, go to the left. Look out for the fireballs, or they'll flame you from the back. Go down the first well you come to. Take the first exit on the right. This will bring you to another well. Jump in. Then take the exit on the right (the first one). You will be in a room with blue goblins. Mosey down the hallway until you come to the bricks that move and jump on them to be carried up five levels. Don't take any exits while you are still on these stairs.

Once you get to the top of the stairs, go left and keep going until you see the elevator. Jump into the elevator and ride it to the top. Kill the blue snake and go left. At the end of the passage, say hello to Rohpah on top of a well. Go down the well and get out on the first exit you come to in the well. There will be another well on the right. Jump down it, exit, and go all the way to the bottom. Once there, go to the right of the screen into the area with the crabs.

When you kill the crabs, you'll get some hearts. Keep going right and go down the well at the end. Go to the bottom of that well and then left. There's a Red Knight and a red snake at the end of the hallway. The dragon's lair is just on the next screen. To go in, knock on the red door. Smack the dragon on the head to kill him. You're a hero!

More Power Pointers

- After you get your first sword, press pause 73 times and you'll get 45 pieces of gold.

- Always go to the hospital if you can, especially if you have some coins to revitalize your hearts and get some time.

- It's fun to go into rooms (such as the tavern or fortune teller's room) to see what they say. Some have really good hints and are worth the stop. You need the right goods to get the fortune teller to soothsay.

- Buy a drink in the tavern. You'll get power and sometimes a special hint from the barkeep. Try two drinks for a different outcome.

- If you find yourself in a room with a boss, don't try to make a break for it. You can't get out. You have to do away with the boss, then you get a prize like a better sword or a good key.

Manufacturer Information

Company: Sega of America, Inc.

Address: P.O. Box 2167
South San Francisco, CA
94080

Game Counselor Hot Line: 415-871-GAME
(Please remember this is a regular toll charge telephone call.) 6 a.m. to 8:45 p.m. Pacific Time Monday through Friday and 8 a.m. to 5:45 p.m. Pacific Time Saturday and Sunday

Typical Price: $37.99